DECK
IDEAS YOU CAN USE

UPDATED EDITION

STUNNING DESIGNS & FANTASTIC FEATURES **FOR YOUR DREAM DECK**

CHRIS PETERSON

Cool Springs Press

Home and Garden Experts™

MINNEAPOLIS, MINNESOTA

Quarto is the authority on a wide range of topics.
Quarto educates, entertains and enriches the lives of our readers—enthusiasts and lovers of hands-on living.
www.quartoknows.com

First published in 2011 by Cool Springs Press, an imprint of Quarto Publishing Group USA Inc., 400 First Avenue North, Suite 400, Minneapolis, MN 55401 USA. This edition published 2016.
Telephone: (612) 344-8100 Fax: (612) 344-8692

quartoknows.com
Visit our blogs at quartoknows.com

Cool Springs Press titles are also available at discounts in bulk quantity for industrial or sales-promotional use. For details contact the Special Sales Manager at Quarto Publishing Group USA Inc., 400 First Avenue North, Suite 400, Minneapolis, MN 55401 USA.

10 9 8 7 6 5 4

ISBN: 978-1-59186-653-4

Library of Congress Cataloging-in-Publication Data

Peterson, Chris, 1961-
Deck ideas you can use : stunning designs & fantastic features for your dream deck / by Chris Peterson. -- Updated edition.
pages cm
ISBN 978-1-59186-653-4 (paperback)
1. Decks (Architecture, Domestic) I. Title.
TH4970.P474 2015
690'.184--dc23
2015020665

Acquiring Editor: Mark Johanson
Project Manager: Alyssa Bluhm
Art Director: Brad Springer
Cover Designer: Kent Jensen
Layout: Rebecca Pagel

Printed in China

CONTENTS

INTRODUCTION

Exploit modern materials with the newest decking innovation—cellular PVC. Strong, stain- and scratch-resistant, and available in the same wide range of surface looks and colors that composites are, this material is quickly becoming a popular deck material option. PVC decking makes it easy to design special features and shapes like the eye-catching curves in this deck. And it's just as low-maintenance as you would expect a synthetic material to be.

Decks are an indelible part of the North American suburban (and, increasingly, urban) landscape. They are incredibly popular not only because they are reasonably easy to build or have built, but mostly because they extend living space outside like no other surface. They are incredibly versatile structures that are easy to design and customize according to your particular preferences and the way you want to enjoy your outdoor spaces. Any new deck design is limited to a degree by property boundaries and basic codes, regulations, and existing yard features. For instance, you should never build a deck over a septic drain field. However, within these boundaries, the sky is the limit.

The potential, in any case, is amazing. Are you looking for a simple outdoor platform where you can relax and read in good weather? That's easy enough. Or perhaps you have more of a stage in mind, a place where you can cook out for special occasions and throw parties during summer weekends? Consider an outdoor kitchen with a built-in breakfast bar like the one on page 100. Have you always dreamed of soaking your aches away in a bubbling jetted spa tub? You'll enjoy an embarrassment of riches when it comes to picking one out, with many choices shown on pages 81 to 85. How about a fire pit for enchanting, mood-setting, nighttime gatherings? You'll find the latest innovations in outdoor flame holders on pages 155 to 157. No matter what you want to add to your deck, you'll discover the full range of possibilities vividly illustrated throughout this book.

You'll also learn about the many materials available to create your dream deck. You may be a purist who wants a redwood structure that will age to a charming gray. Or perhaps you prefer the modern alternative of a composite or cellular PVC deck for low maintenance and longevity. Either way, you can check out the vast number of looks available starting on page 17.

You don't even have to be seeking something particular when you're browsing these pages. *Deck Ideas You Can Use* can serve just as well as a dream guide to what might be your own backyard oasis. The first step, as always, is to dive in, and get dreaming, thinking, planning, and moving toward your ultimate outdoor platform.

Create multiple outdoor "rooms" with a multilevel deck. Although a multilevel design requires more planning, expertise, and expense, it also makes the deck exponentially more usable and is especially ideal for a sloping yard. Define different areas by the features you place there, positioned according to what makes sense. This deck's upper level has been divided into dining and casual seating areas, close to the kitchen. The hot tub has been positioned on a lower level, where its weight is more easily supported, and the tub is accessible from the pool.

Merge your deck fluidly with the house structure. This modest, ground-level backyard deck tucks in attractively next to a bump-out in the architecture. The white vinyl decking not only provides a low-maintenance deck surface, it also matches the home's siding. Use low-growing foundation plantings, like the plants bordering the perimeter of this deck, to further blend the surface into its surroundings.

Take design cues from the house shape to meld the deck with the home. The semicircular shape of this deck mimics the arcing brick bump-out on the back of this house, creating an inviting semicircle that opens out into the yard. The deck visually nests into an inside corner, and the color of the composite decking complements that of the house siding and trim.

Have an idea of what you want to showcase—garden features, a pool, a view, or the deck itself—before you settle on a final deck design. This deck sits at ground level, creating a handsome area right next to a pool. Entirely waterproof, the composite decking is ideal for a site such as this, and the neutral color allows the alluring blue of the pool to dominate the backyard setting.

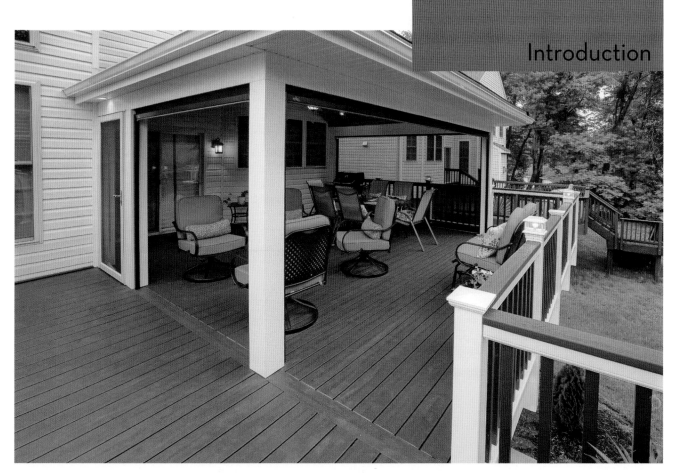

Expand a porch with a deck of the same material. These homeowners replaced the existing porch decking with the decking they used in constructing a two-sided expansion. The result is a seamless structure that looks entirely natural. White posts and top rails in the deck railings match the porch roof posts and the color of the home's siding, reinforcing the integrated nature of the design.

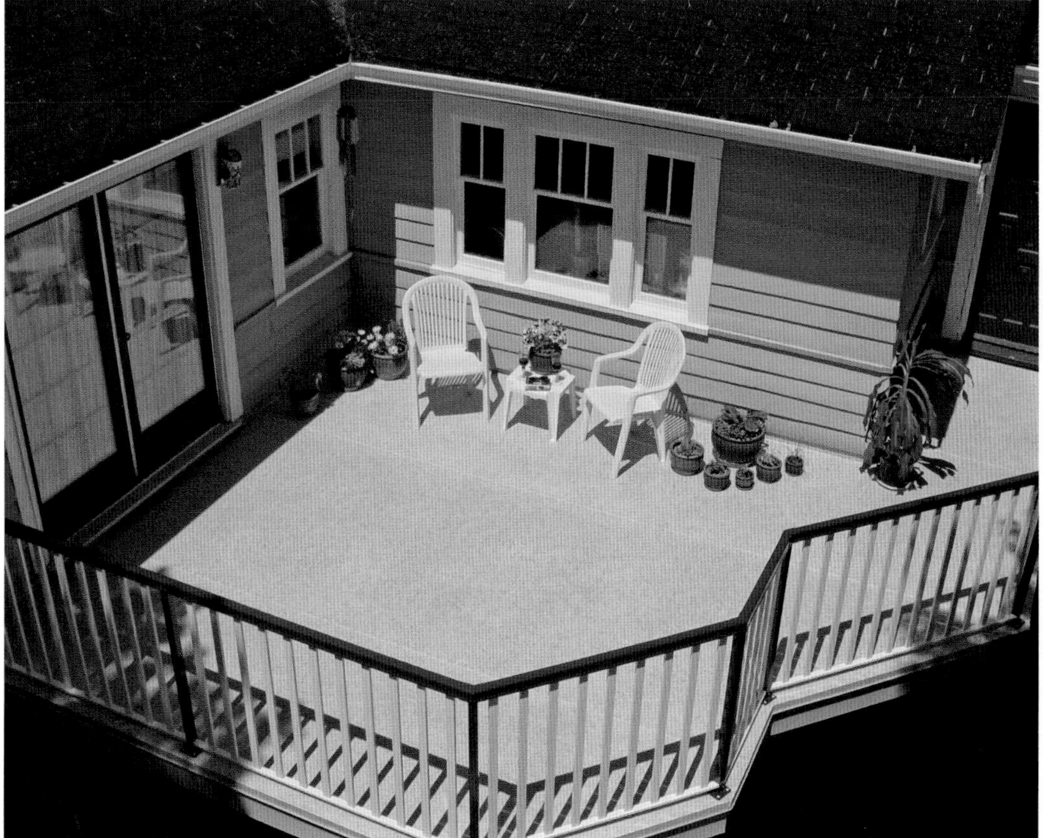

Reimagine your deck surface in a whole new material. Thanks to advances in vinyl technology, you'll find amazing alternatives to traditional board decking. Surfaces such as the one shown here are low maintenance, durable, and water resistant. The vinyl is rendered in a range of appearances from stone to the solid-sheet look on this elevated deck. The company that makes this surface provides everything you'll need for installation except a backyard.

Build around nature to create a deck that blends with the landscape and scenery, rather than fights with it. Accommodating nature can be as simple as shaping the deck's border to run around an old-growth shrub or as complex as cutting a hole right in the middle of the deck surface to accommodate a long-standing evergreen that grows close to the house.

Introduction

Exploit existing technology for a luxury showcase deck. The elegant dark brown decking that forms the base of this impressive outdoor space is the cutting edge of composites. Available in a range of tones, completely waterproof, and stain- and fade-resistant, it is also incredibly durable. You can use it in good conscience because it's made from 95 percent recycled content. A material like this is well accented by a custom overhang and high-end outdoor fan-light fixtures.

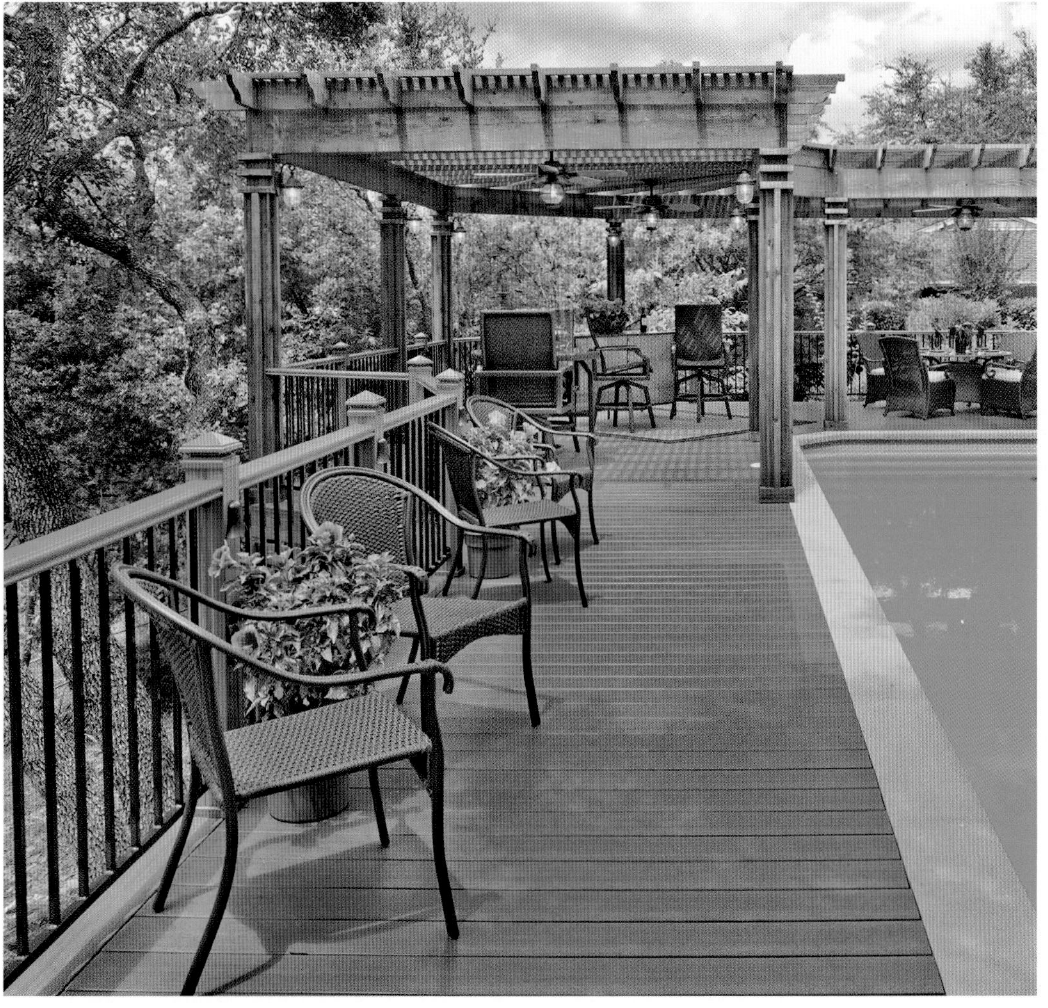

Use a poolside deck as a fantastic opportunity to go beyond the staid traditional stone patio surface. The deck around this pool spells luxury with a capital L, including two built-in pergolas that define and separate sitting and dining areas. The rest of the deck is left uncovered to allow for unrestricted sunbathing, and to exploit an incredible wooded vista on the other side.

Make a standout spa tub the star of the show by centering it on a modest deck. The deck boards that frame this luxurious tub were chosen to blend in with the surroundings, to make the tub look like it is part of the natural environment. The directional pattern of the boards was specifically designed to draw the eye inward toward the water feature.

Use a deck to turn a beautiful view into a usable sanctuary. This bilevel lower deck transformed a large, densely forested, hilly backyard into a secluded outdoor hideaway perfect for recharging your batteries and entertaining well away from the pressures of the outside world. Subtle but effective wired-in lighting makes the space enjoyable night or day, and complementary browns in the border boards, level transition, and field of the deck provide a measure of visual interest while blending into the surroundings.

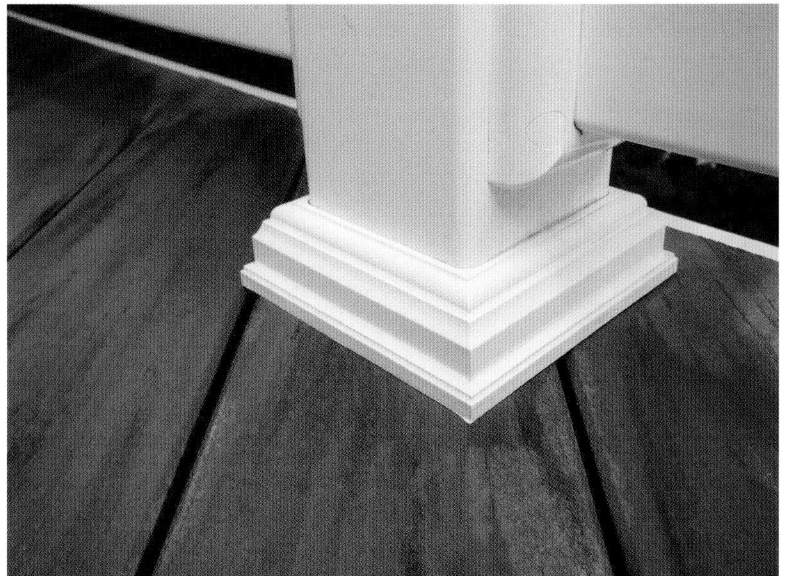

Introduction

Make even a small deck special by using standout materials and fine architectural details. The designer of this deck achieved a stunning look with the grain and color of ipe hardwood used in the deck surface. He accented that beauty with a finely detailed post molding that replicates the appearance of a milled footing.

Please the eye with curving shapes. Curves are naturally attractive and graphically intriguing and often suit landscaped yards better than a square or rectangle would. In addition to creating a pleasing shape, the designer of this deck used white composite legs for the benches, making them stand up visually as well as physically. The benches also provide an obvious border element, creating a more defined and formal separation between house and lawn.

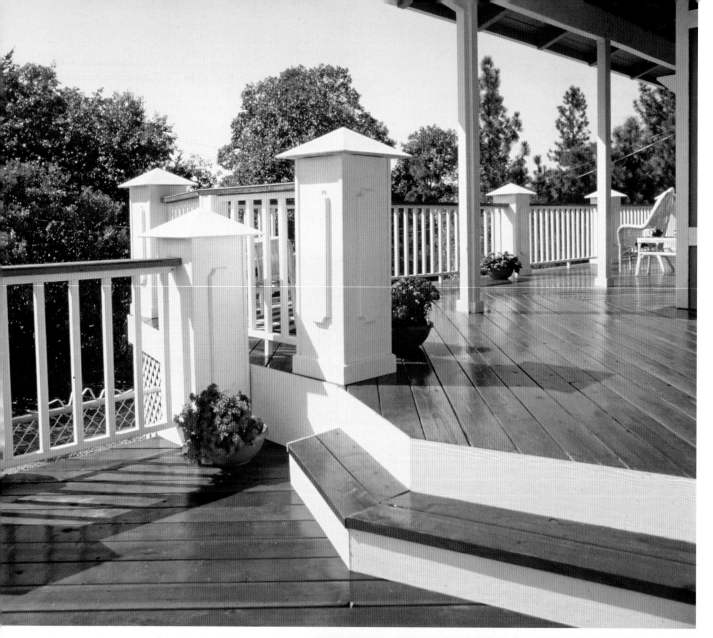

Use contrast as a powerful design tool. The secret is to never overwhelm the look of the deck with jarring juxtapositions between contrasting materials and colors. The unique appearance of this redwood decking is set off by sparkling, bright white railings and stair risers. White is a great accent or detail color for most decks, creating a sharp, clean look against most types and colors of decking. White risers are practical as well, providing a visual depth indicator to prevent tripping when the sky is overcast, or at night.

Integrate old and new structures to avoid a deck that looks tacked-on. This older brick house is perfectly complemented by the composite deck, which was designed as an extension of the existing porch. A border of lighter colored boards establishes the connection with the porch, and the color of the decking and railings works well with the brick façade.

Build in a bump-out to keep seating or other deck features out of traffic flow. This is a particularly effective strategy on smaller decks, where furniture can often cramp movement, making the deck less comfortable to use. A rectangular bump-out like this one is fairly easy to design into the plans for the deck. However, you can add a lot of visual interest with an octagonal or curving bump-out—a good option to consider if you've got a pro building your deck.

Accent a deck with built-in structures wherever possible to make the entire surface more welcoming. Simple built-in benches such as these corner units add a bit of visual flair and increase the usability of the deck. This corner left bare would have been boring and visual dead space. Throw pillows in weatherproof outdoor fabrics are a great low-cost way to dress up built-in seating on a deck.

Design your deck to exploit yard features. Decks are amazingly adaptable when you're careful to work out the design shape and elevations. The mostly unusable slope in this large yard becomes a wonderful, eye-catching background to stadium-style deck steps that follow the slope's natural rise. The steps can be used as additional seating as need arises, and a contrasting lip trim adds visual flair. The entire design maintains an open and airy aspect that is remarkably inviting.

Run your decking through rocks for a rustic appeal. Crushed stone, river pebbles, lava rock, or the small boulders in this landscape all marry wonderfully with a simple deck surface. The natural-looking tones of this cellular PVC product mimics the shades of stone and plants all around, helping blend the linear deck into the more abstract surroundings.

Dine worry-free on a composite deck. One of the great aspects of installing composite decking is that cleanup is a breeze. This decking is made from 100 percent recycled carpet fibers and is impervious to insects such as termites, as well as stains from food and wine. It's easy to maintain and best of all, it looks just like real wood.

Introduce fabrics to bring luxury to your deck. A rather plain view is dressed up with the many textures scattered around this simple backyard deck. Glass partition railings add a sleek element, and removable overhang features canvas drapes that can be closed to create an intimate space when necessary. Upholstered cushions provide invitingly soft surfaces that promote lounging and socializing. The look is also incredibly upscale.

DECKING MATERIALS

The materials you choose for your deck have a huge effect on cost, appearance, longevity, and maintenance. Select carefully to get the best value for your money. Once upon a time, all decks were either hardwood or softwood. Hardwoods remain exotic and expensive options, but are long lasting, pest- and rot-resistant, and offer incredible appearances. Redwood and cedar are the most popular choices among softwoods. Both are sturdy, unappealing to insects, and beautiful, but require regular maintenance. Pressure-treated wood is most often pine and is impregnated with chemicals that protect against insects and rot.

Synthetics have largely taken over the new deck market. These options include composites incorporating recycled wood and plastics in engineered lumber, pure plastic boards made of PVC or vinyl, and other variations. Generally, synthetic decking is incredibly durable and long-lasting, easy to clean, and relatively inexpensive. The boards and railings usually mimic the look and texture of wood. More expensive versions create a more convincing illusion and offer added protection against UV rays and stains.

You can also opt for metal—specifically aluminum—at the low end of the price scale. Newer versions improve on the unappealing sound and quickly degrading finishes that plagued older aluminum decking. The newest decking material is an adaptation from patios. Manufacturers are creating systems whereby stone and other non-traditional deck surfaces can be laid to look almost like a patio but with the framework and elevation of a deck. Some produce sheet vinyl that opens up the potential for unusual looking, one-of-a-kind deck surfaces.

Fake it convincingly with the latest composites. This deck may look like it was constructed of walnut lumber, but it is actually a composite that is highly resistant to stains, scratches, splits, mildew, and mold. It is water- and insect-proof as well. The lumber is engineered with grooves that allow it to be attached with hidden fasteners, making the look even more attractive. You'll find composites in a wide range of hardwood and softwood appearances.

Redwood

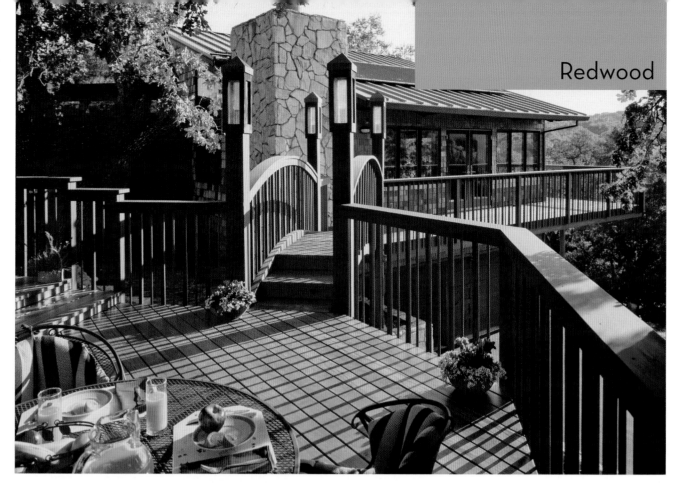

Say "magnificent" in your deck design by leveraging the glory of redwood. High-end, upscale deck installations are perfect places to show redwood decking to its best advantage. The natural elegance of the wood's surface is the ideal complement to stately features like the thick railing and impressive lantern posts on the bridge of this deck.

Redwood is a natural choice for pool decking. Heart grades resist moisture and rot, and any redwood takes stains and finishes as well as, or better than, any other softwood. This elegant deck provides a walkway around a pool, complementing a stone border and adding fascinating detail with grain and deep color that draws the eye.

Choose a redwood finish that suits your tastes and design goals. Although the wood is renowned for its lovely natural appearance, redwood can also be stained or painted. The gray of this deck perfectly complements the house's siding and seals the redwood in a way that ensures the surface will hold up well over time. A bright white pergola and railings provide some visual pop, and ensure that the deck doesn't fade into a ho-hum neutral look.

Vary the material or finish you use to increase visual interest. Different features on the deck—even built-ins—don't necessarily have to be crafted from the same wood, or same grade, that the deck itself is. This outdoor space makes good use of a little variety. The pergola, built-in planters and seating are all sealed to retain the eye-catching color of the wood. The decking has been left unfinished so that the color fades to gray as the wood ages.

Make the most of redwood's natural allure by nestling a deck in a woodsy setting. Nowhere is a redwood deck more at home than under a copse of trees on an untamed woodsy hillside. This deck provides wonderful outdoor space on a previously unusable slope, and seems to meld into the earth tones surrounding it. The underlying support structure was built of less attractive and less expensive pressure-treated lumber. Redwood fascia boards and lattice skirting ensure the alluring color and patterns of the redwood dominate.

Redwood is regional. The cost and availability of redwood varies according to your locale. It is plentiful and relatively affordable on the West Coast and in the Pacific Northwest.

Use redwood for angled decks to make every facet beautiful. Because even cut edges of a natural wood like redwood are attractive, angled portions of a deck don't expose any odd-looking edges. It's also easier to design in angles such as these, than to create long curves with redwood. In any case, the angles are an interesting and energized look, one that also offers a customized sitting area that perfectly fits in an odd location like a rocky outcropping.

Elevate the impression of a modest desk by building it purely of redwood. This simple two-level structure impresses with the beauty of the wood finished natural, and a central octagon deck shape design for the upper level. There isn't a lot of fancy detailing, but it isn't really needed for this structure to be a stunner.

Pair redwood with a spa tub for a natural marriage that looks like it was made in heaven. The unmistakable beauty of real redwood provides the perfect backdrop for a luxurious outdoor spa. The large tub here has been positioned as the centerpiece of the deck, a place where the homeowners can unwind after a long day, looking out over an expertly landscaped yard. The "clear heart" rated boards used here not only offer an unrivaled appearance relatively free of knots and imperfections, they also resist rot and insects.

Simplify to exploit the inherent beauty in redwood decking. If you're going to use redwood in its natural state, you can make the most of the distinctive appearance by avoiding highly detailed railings, lighting fixtures, or other features in different materials. The look becomes unified when the wood forms most of the entire deck structure, as it does in this sprawling multilevel construction. With a material as beautiful as redwood, you don't need much more for a stunning look.

Paint cedar where you want a clean, sharp, stately appearance. As this majestic elevated deck proves, you don't necessarily need to rely solely on the cedar's grain or color for a stunning outdoor structure. Cedar takes both stain and paint well. White fascia and support-beam trim look crisp, and cladding the support beams in vinyl that looks like millwork turns functional elements into arresting design focal points.

Create constant fascination underfoot by exploiting cedar's graining. Cedar offers surface patterns and a deep rich color unlike any other wood. The designer of this deck added even more visual interest by running the boards of the lower deck on diagonal, which adds visual flair. Cedar is so beautiful that builders usually use the same wood for the railings as well as the surface.

Use cedar in place of redwood for comparable insect and rot resistance. Cedar offers a lighter and browner color but is lightweight and easy to work with. It doesn't check or split and is slightly less expensive than redwood (which is not always widely available). Left natural, as it has been on this deck, the wood will eventually weather to a gray similar to aging redwood.

Complement siding of just about any color or material with cedar. It features a naturally harmonious shade of brown and blends with practically any style of landscaping. Cedar is also a very forgiving lumber that you can use to build many types of deck accessories and furnishings to match, such as the built-in bench and overhead arbor adorning this deck.

Use pressure-treated wood for ground-level decks. The wood is also sturdy enough for support structures, such as the modest pergola and benches that border this deck. Regardless of the material, though, designing a deck to sit at an angle to the house is a great way to make what might otherwise be a plain structure much more visually interesting. Let treated lumber acclimate for a few days—it is prone to wood movement, twisting, and warping.

Improve the appearance of pressure-treated decking with stain or paint. By choosing a shade very similar to the siding, the homeowner who built this deck made sure that the deck blends seamlessly with the house. A built-in bench adds style, and running boards in three different directions on two different levels adds even more panache.

Pressure-Treated Wood

Bring the grain of pressure-treated Southern pine to life with a light stain. Although railings are often crafted of different wood or stained in a different shade, the builder of this bilevel deck stained all the wood the same. The effect gives the look continuity, making it easy on the eyes.

Save money with pressure-treated decking without sacrificing design. The recreational platform in this photo includes built-in seating with a louvered pergola, planter boxes, detailed fencing, and lattice skirting, at a fraction of what hardwood construction would have cost.

Showcase elegance in a fine-grained cumaru dining deck accented by chic glass railing inserts. Cumaru is not only an incredibly beautiful hardwood, it is also dense and strong enough to last decades. Reputable suppliers only sell cumaru taken from certified sustainable forests. That means that it is a great environmentally responsible choice for the homeowner who's looking to build a deck out of drop-dead gorgeous wood.

Hardwoods

Tap the power of cumaru, an incredibly durable hardwood. It has a dense structure that resists moisture, insects, rot, and mold. It's an ideal wood for high-traffic deck stairs like these, leading from a back door used as a primary entrance to a cumaru deck. This beautiful wood can be left unfinished, in which case it will age to a lovely gray. Sealed, it will remain the dynamic brown shown here.

Grace a deck with the magical, honey-amber shades of garapa. Also known as Brazilian ash, clear heart garapa is the most common quality garapa used, ensuring that there are no knots or imperfections to mar the enchanting surface color. This deck has been finished in a clear, penetrating, oil-based sealer that maintains the original color. Notice the builder used steel post-and-beam supports that are visually unobtrusive and tie the deck and pergola to the modern architecture of the house.

Contrast the intriguing chocolate brown of ipe hardwood decking with crisp white. The introduction of bright white helps accentuate the fine grain and lush color of the hardwood. The railings and fascia boards are made from composite materials; using less expensive materials for details like these goes a long way toward cutting the overall cost of a hardwood deck.

Combine dramatic deck designs with the stunning appearance of an exotic hardwood. Ipe was used in this deck, including the steep terraces and angled stairs, to contrast the modern architecture's siding. The color of the hardwood complements splashes of brown in the stone used for the patio. The shapes of the deck structure interestingly contrast the lower surface.

Hardwoods

Meld a deck into thick exotic plantings, by using a dark hardwood surface. The look of this deck fits perfectly with the jungle flora that has been used in the backyard landscaping. It also complements the rough brick pavers and wrought iron fixtures. Matching deck material to other decorative elements and plantings ensures that the structure doesn't stick out like a sore thumb.

Mix board direction and grain pattern to ignite visual dynamite. The undulating pattern of the tigerwood in this deck not only grabs attention, it is also a low-maintenance option that costs less than many other hardwoods. The wood features an absolutely riveting deep golden-brown base color with darker brown or black striping throughout. This deck makes great use of the wood's patterns, with boards running toward a diamond inlay centerpiece. Create this sort of visual interest and you may find guests on the deck spending more time looking down than checking out the view.

Glimmer with garapa. An exotic "ironwood" like garapa is truly impressive when you use it to craft an entire deck—including railings, fascia, and steps. The hardwood comes alive with shimmering golden tones that are unmistakable and distinctively unique. A look like this is not inexpensive to achieve, but it is unforgettable and long-lasting. Furnish a deck like this carefully, to allow the surface to shine through as much as possible.

Keep hardwood decking pristine. If you're going to the expense and effort to install a stunningly beautiful hardwood surface such as this, it makes no sense to ruin the look with screwheads along each board. This supplier provides a "vanishing" system of fasteners, allowing installation without face screwing or nailing. The result speaks for itself. Because hardwoods tend to expand and contract less than other types of decking, the boards can be installed relatively snug for a nearly gapless appearance.

Exploit board variations for an authentic look. Never shy away from leveraging the differences board to board, among hardwood decking. Varying shades and graining patterns are what give hardwood deck surfaces their undeniable character and allure. Choosing boards that are too similar can diminish the alluring appearance—especially with woods like the hardwood used in this deck—featuring exceptional variations.

Inset: Match accessories to the look of the hardwood for the most attractive overall design. The ipe wood used in this deck is a midrange to dark wood with tight graining. The wood marries perfectly with black post-cap lights and rail balusters. White or even rust-red accents would not have worked as well with the wood's color and grain patterns.

Use composite decking in an exposed, sun-drenched location for a textured, splinter-free, durable surface. Most composites and PVC decking are prone to a modest amount of fading under prolonged direct sun exposure, but manufacturers are increasingly formulating their products to hold up under even the toughest conditions, without deterioration or obvious discoloration.

Go seamless by using hidden fasteners with your composite deck. Attachments such as the ones shown here allow you to create a clean, sleek appearance on the deck surface, with boards spaced extremely close together and no visible screw or nail heads showing that would mar the deck surface.

Composites

Enjoy hardwood for a lower cost. A Brazilian cherry deck underfoot? Not quite. It's a composite that matches that intriguing hardwood's distinctive appearance to a T, but beats the cost by a mile. Hidden fasteners ensure that the deck is as handsome as can be, and the natural resistance to elements and wear and tear guarantee that this deck will continue to look like elegant hardwood for years to come.

Fight mold, rot, moisture infiltration, and splintering. Composite decking's durability and damage resistance make it ideal for a multipurpose structure such as this backyard retreat, where water will be splashed and bare feet are the order of the day. Most composites are also easy to clean, making spills a breeze to deal with. And, as this image illustrates, the material is no slouch in the looks department either.

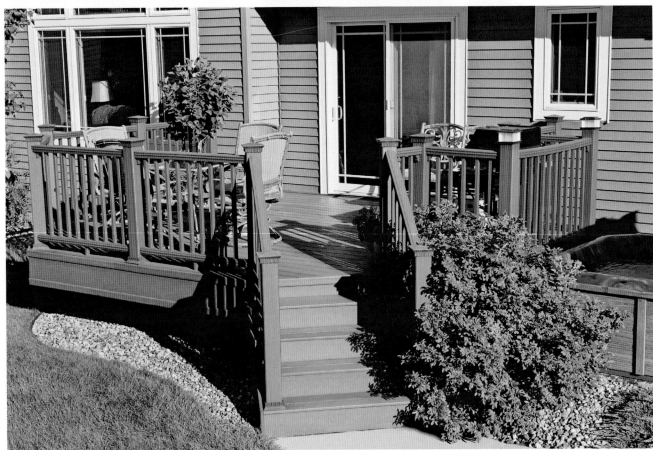

Go monochromatic with composites. The material is perfect for a unified look such as the appearance on this small deck, where color variations would stand out like a sore thumb. Accent details, like the post-cap lights here that illuminate a spa tub mounted on its own concrete footing, can be added for more visual interest.

Choose composites for curved or unusual shapes in deck boards. Manufacturers can customize the deck boards to suit a designer's needs. As this photo shows, an elegant curve can be easily added to the deck surface. You can also see the color, grain, and texture of the composite boards, fabricated to mimic real wood.

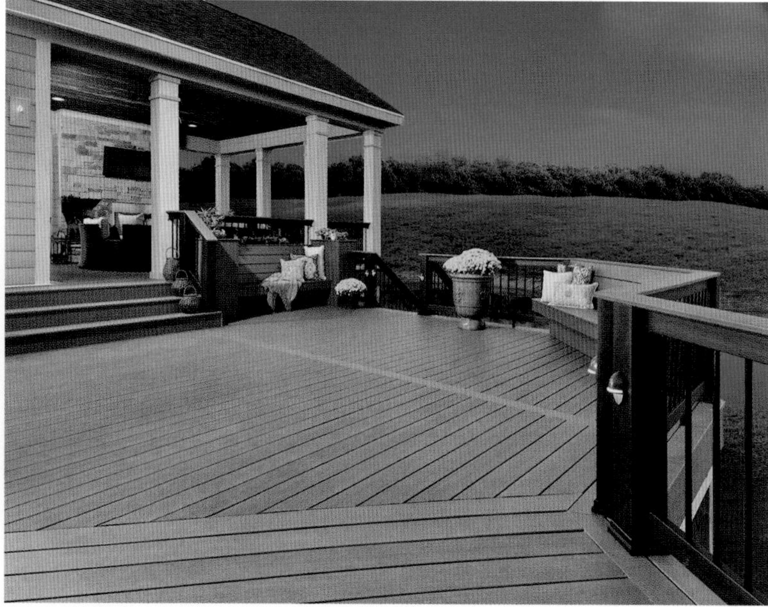

Exploit technology with capped composites. This beautiful deck is built of composite decking that has been "capped" with a thermal plastic layer, increasing durability and stain- and scratch-resistance. The material is available in the same diversity of surface appearances as standard composites, at a slightly higher price. It's a great option for a high-traffic deck surface that will maintain a just-built look over time.

Blend composites with colored hardware. Although composite decking is often installed with hidden fasteners, you can achieve almost the same seamless look with specialty screws that have colored heads. The heads disappear into the surface of the deck, allowing the beauty of the composite material to shine.

Vary the look of your deck with modern composites. Unlike early generations of this product, contemporary composite decking features amazing diversity board to board. This makes the material look more like real wood, creating the kind of masterful appearance that this deck boasts. The finish and unique grain patterns across the surface of the deck fools the eye into thinking this is real wood, while the synthetic material ensures deck durability and requires only modest maintenance.

Create a unique illusion with the right composite. This decking was developed to convincingly look like weathered redwood or cedar deck boards. The understated gray color also blends well with surrounding colors and elements, including dense landscaping, a black railing, and brick house siding. The color won't fade and cooking messes are easy to clean up off the surface.

Choose from a vast range of colors, textures, and grain patterns. Many composite products mimic expensive hardwoods, such as this deck that looks convincingly like a tropical ironwood, such as garapa. Even with modest fading, this deck will look like a much more expensive wood structure for decades to come, all with the minimal maintenance of two to three cleanings per year.

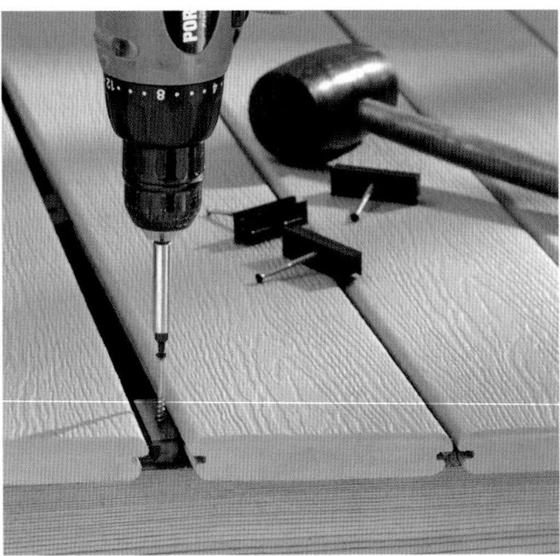

Conceal fasteners for the most flawless appearance. Many composite boards are fabricated with side-edge grooves that can be used in tandem with groove fasteners, for a top surface that is not blemished with screw heads. Installing hidden groove fasteners is an easy and quick process, and composite decking manufacturers often supply the fasteners with their products. Hidden fasteners are also every bit as secure as face screws.

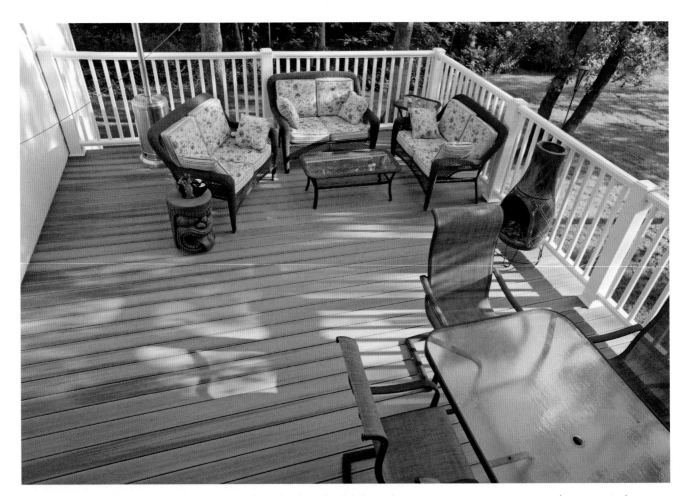

Try "teak" for a tantalizing deck surface. Although darker hardwood and darker colors are more common, a composite that mimics teak can be an incredibly beautiful deck surface, especially when accented with a white railing and placed next to a light-colored house wall. The stain-resistance of composite materials means that the surface won't be easily discolored and will remain this stunning for a long time to come.

Composites

Eat and drink worry free on a composite deck. High-quality composites are stain- and moisture-resistant. A spill like this can be cleaned up even after it has sat for minutes. This aspect of composites makes the material a favorite for decking under an outdoor kitchen but is equally good for backyard decks regularly used for cocktails and snacks.

Define deck areas with a two-tone design. One of the wonderful things about composite decking is that ordering two different colors incurs no additional expense. That means you can outline deck areas in different colors, such as the tan used on this multilevel deck. Color variations not only add a crisp visual element to the structure, they also offer the practical benefit of ensuring against trips in low-light circumstances.

Color-coordinate your deck with composites. Bring the look of your deck together with borders, field boards, fascia, and railings in the same family of hues. The tans and browns of this deck are a perfect example of what you can accomplish by ordering all the deck components from one supplier and carefully blending shades so that the entire structure looks natural and pleasing to the eye.

Fight moisture with the right composite. Different composite materials are formulated to have different strengths and weaknesses. This particular product boasts incredible moisture resistance, making it ideal for situations where water is a near constant—such as the lakefront and rainy forest setting of this extended deck. Buying the right composite for your situation is the way to get the most out of your decking dollar.

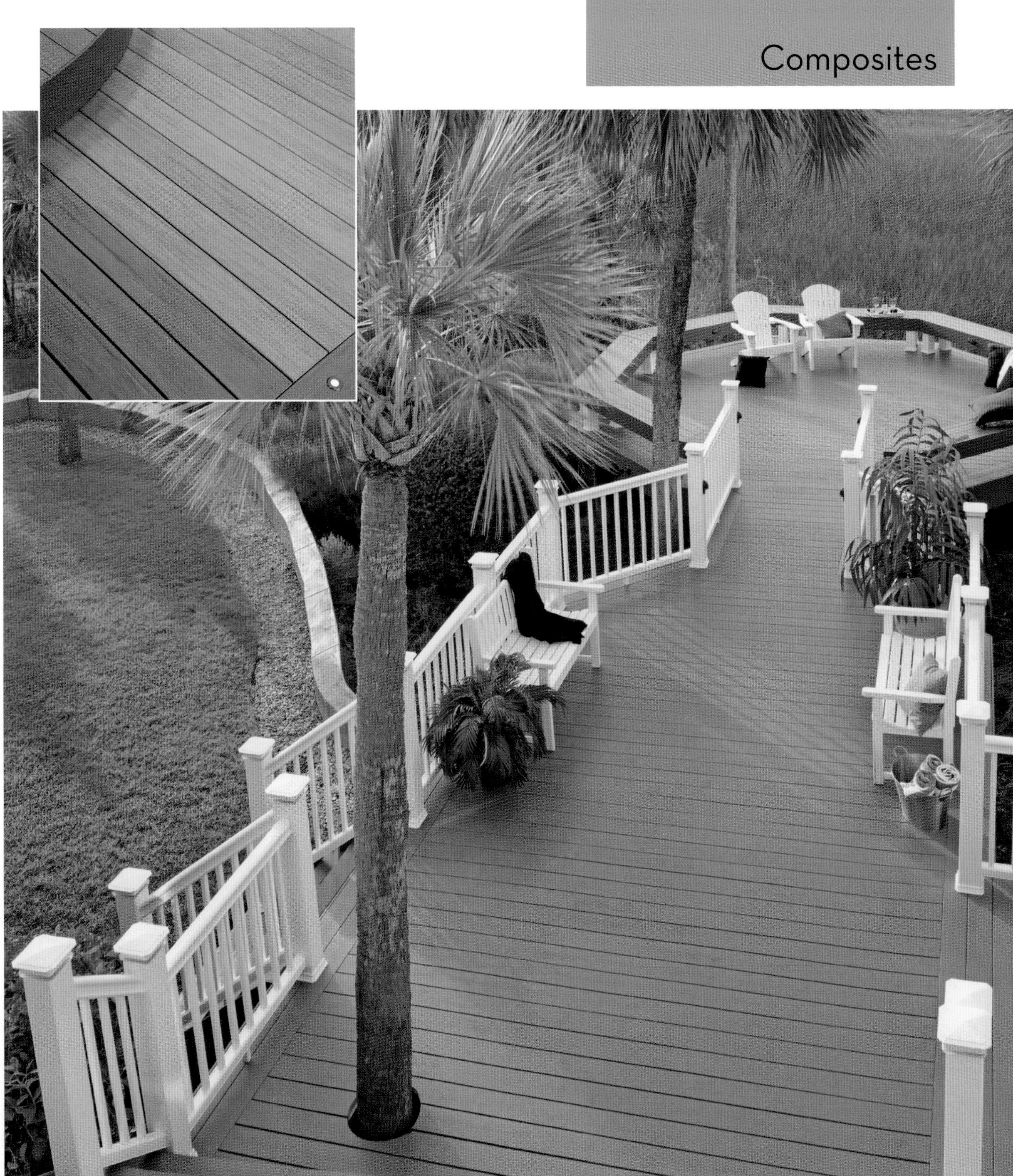

Go gray-and-white for a classic appeal. The color scheme of this composite deck is at once stately and fresh. It stands out from the lush surrounding vegetation without being jarring to the eye. The white railings help distinguish the deck surface from surrounding areas in the dark, and the octagon formed by benches that match the deck color are an excellent finishing touch on what is a very classy construction.

Inset: Mix and match to add visual interest in your composite deck. Although homeowners commonly choose one shade of composite decking for their deck, the availability of multiple colors for the same price opens up a variety of design options. Here, a two-tone deck surface creates a wonderful contrast over the span of the deck and establishes an unusual design twist that really sets the deck apart.

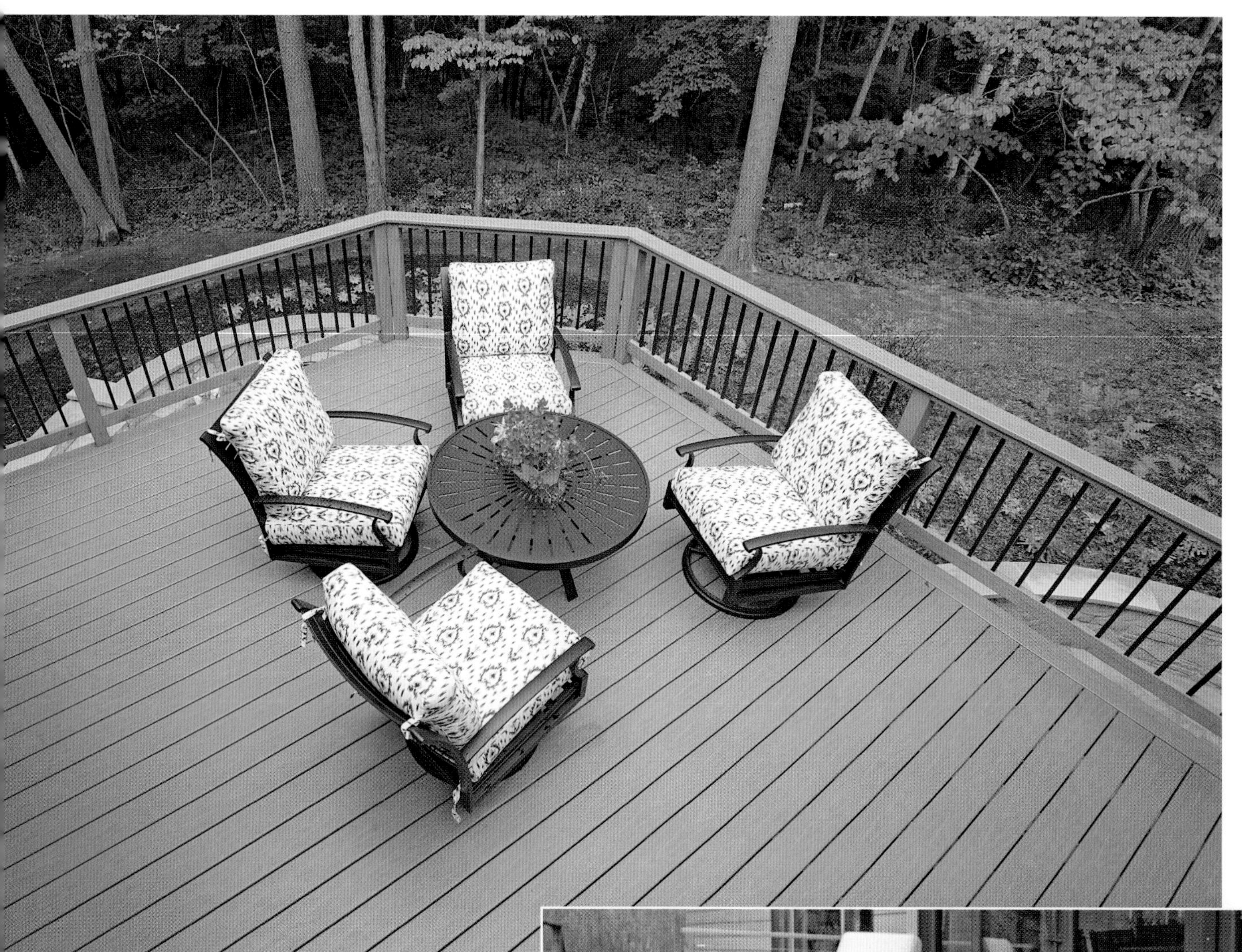

Work a wood look into your deck surface with high-end PVC decking. As with composites, PVC manufacturers have mastered the art of creating incredibly realistic imitations of natural materials. A close look at this decking shows just how fine that art is. These deck boards are hard to distinguish from actual walnut—except that they'll last longer with less maintenance and at a lower cost!

Invest in a durable surface by installing a PVC deck. Beautiful? You bet. But a backyard deck like this, built of PVC decking installed with hidden fasteners, is also incredibly tough. It will hold up well to the elements, resist stains, and stand up against physical damage such as scratching and basic wear and tear.

Keep on cooking as long as you have PVC underfoot. Like its relative, composites, PVC decking is tough enough to hold up to hot foods and beverages. More importantly, the material resists stains from red wine to blueberry cobbler to your favorite barbecued ribs.

Ensure against rot and moisture problems. A deck location such as this—hugging the ground around water-loving plants in a rainy part of the country—can put any deck surface to the test. But PVC passes with flying colors. Not only is the material fairly immune to damage from water, it is also mold- and mildew-resistant. Here, PVC's ease of fabrication and durability create a lovely, irregular-shaped deck.

Turn to PVC decking for the unusual and eye-catching. Manufacturers have produced an incredibly varied selection of decking color and looks. The "hazelwood" show here is one of the most stunning. Its light color is best accented with darker fixtures and accents, but no matter what you put on it or around it, the material will remain drop-dead gorgeous for a long time to come.

Turn to synthetics for adaptable uses. PVC, like composites, is an excellent option for crafting deck structures to fit right into the deck surface, such as the bench here. This is a great way to use extra boards in the case of a miscalculation, or just to have comfortable seating with the same durability and low maintenance as the deck surface itself.

Temper lighter-colored decking by bordering with darker elements. Here, a darker house siding on one side and black railings on the other work together to define and provide visual counterpoints to the beige-and-tan deck. The look is appealing and creates a natural and pleasing visual tension.

PVC

Use any kind of furniture your heart desires when your deck is PVC. Tough is the name of the game with this material, and it has a high resistance to scratching. That means you can trot out even your heavy iron outdoor furniture without worries that the feet will scrape the deck and leave ugly marks. The same is true for potted plants and the condensation that often forms under the pots. Not a problem with PVC.

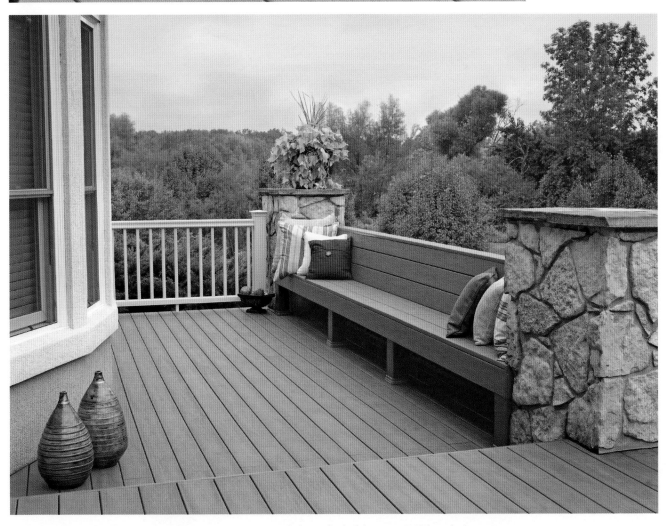

Make built-ins with PVC. Seats and other structures can easily be crafted of the same PVC boards that go into the deck itself. This bench integrates perfectly with the deck because the same boards and surface finish has been used. The material is also pleasant to the touch—no worry about splinters! However, whenever you're creating built-ins from the same material used in the deck, add fine details like the footings on this bench. Details like this create flair and protect against a boring sameness.

Dine in elevated splendor with the help of aluminum. Lightweight aluminum decking made this simple deck quicker, easier, and less expensive to build than it would have been using another decking material. It's also a fire-resistant option that won't warp, bow, or split. Not to mention the colors perfectly complement the color of the home's siding.

Deal with an exposed site by exploiting the durability of metal. The coating used on this aluminum deck not only comes in a variety of colors, as well as wood-grained options, it is also fade- and slip-resistant. Aluminum does require ample structural support, which is supplied in this case courtesy of pressure-treated members that can be seen between the staircase tread risers.

Aluminum

Match the decking material to the location. An aluminum deck was a good choice for this lakefront home. The decking is water- (even salt water) and mold-resistant and won't rot or rust. The railings are also aluminum, and the homeowner has chosen an elegant color combination of charcoal-gray decking with bright white railings.

Pick aluminum for a modestly sized, ground-level deck. Here, the color and simple shape were chosen to blend in seamlessly with the house and create what is essentially a room without walls. The low-lying structure required modest reinforcement, and rot is not a worry with the aluminum decking. Notice how the homeowner used a rock border in a similar shade to the deck to create a harmonious visual link between deck and yard.

Turn to deck tiles for a quick, simple, and inexpensive option. Although usually used for ground-level surfaces—or preexisting, flat, level, and stable surfaces such as balconies—a tile deck can be customized to just about any linear shape. The homeowner created this simple backyard space with staggered corners to add visual interest.

Craft a lovely secluded space in the garden. An attractive aspect of using deck tiles is the option of playing around with patterns. Here, the deck features simple slatted tiles run in the same direction, with special patterned tiles run in border rows. The variation creates a lot of interest underfoot, and the possibilities for different patterns—from herringbone to entirely unique creations—are almost limitless.

Deck Tiles

Give unsightly, worn surfaces a facelift with deck tiles. The tiles provide an added benefit with their open construction and plastic base that leaves plenty of space for water to drain way. This ensures that the wood does not rot or mold, and keeps the surface from ever becoming too slick. Notice the reducer tiles used around the edge of this pool, creating the look of a custom deck.

Decking tiles are usually produced and sold as square-foot units. Manufacturers offer a selection of hardwoods and composite tiles, and the tiles are produced in simple slatted designs, as shown here, diagonal designs for herringbone patterns, and other board patterns within the single tile. The tiles are normally sold prefinished, requiring only installation.

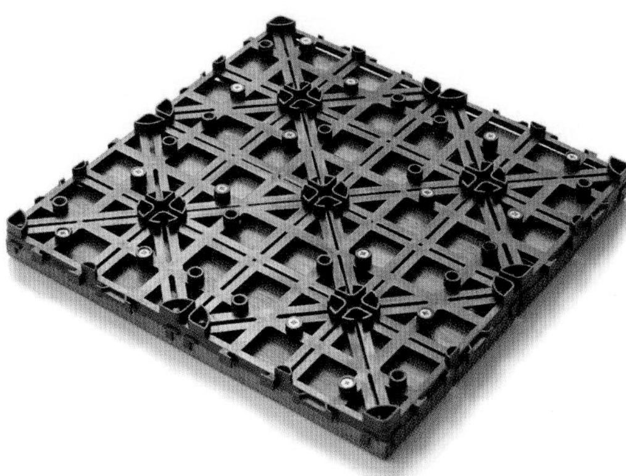

Deck tiles are usually constructed with a plastic base that allows for water drainage and holds the decking material up off the ground. Although connection systems vary from manufacturer to manufacturer, a common method of attachment is plastic tabs that slot into openings on adjacent tiles. This system makes installation extremely easy, requiring no tools in most cases.

Manufacturers produce variations on the basic deck tile to serve in different situations. The side view here is of a "reducer" tile that adds a sloping edge to the border of a deck or over a swimming pool lip. You'll also find special tiles for corners as well as other applications.

Install an elevated "patio" for a second-story surface. The outdoor sitting area shown here features the same substructure as a deck, with a solid subfloor to support tiles, rather than boards. The look is more seamless than board construction, and the possibilities are nearly limitless—the tiled surface can be crafted of stone, vinyl, wood-grained, or other tiles. A sheet vinyl surface can also be installed.

Design a fluid deck that appears all of one piece with a decking alternative. Using a specialized moisture-proof underfloor system, this deck features textured tiles that ensure slipping won't be a problem, especially on the steps that seemed to formed as a single unit with the surface. The mounting and membrane system underneath the deck surface guarantee that water tracked out of the hot tub isn't an issue. This is also an unusual and unique look, one that adds chic to the backyard and tub area.

Non-Traditional Decking

Look beyond the conventional. The specialized system shown here allows homeowners to install a stable, secure, water-resistant, and handsome surface that challenges preconceived notions of what a deck should be. The surface features an attractively mottled appearance, but the mounting system allows the material to be installed in locations normally associated only with board construction. This elevated deck will feature the permanent beauty of stone where a wood or synthetic deck might normally be, offering an intriguing alternative to conventional materials.

IDEAL DECK SIZE AND SHAPE

Deck size and shape are the starting points for your deck's design. That's because deck configuration, and how big or small the structure is, affects how well it serves your needs and fits in with your house and yard. Get the proportions right and the deck will look like it's always been there, and will accommodate whatever uses you have in mind for the space.

Deck size will be constrained to some extent by budget. Other practical concerns will play a part as well. Large landscape features such as old-growth trees may limit how big the deck can be, as will impediments such as severe slopes. Those features will also determine the shape of your deck. Customizing your deck to fit around features in the landscape is a way to make the surface seem a more natural transition between house and yard. But of course, deck shape may also be dictated by other concerns.

Basic squares or rectangles are the easiest—and least expensive—shapes to create. Introduce curves into your deck design and you add visual interest. But severe curves can limit usable space; gentle curves create a more elegant contour. Curves and straight lines are not, however, the only shapes available in deck design. You can choose to design a completely unique shape with unusual angles and polygons to define different areas of the deck.

Deck shapes are really only limited by imagination. Keep in mind, though, that the shape and size of your deck should always be the servant to the way you will use it. No deck design should emphasize look at the cost of function.

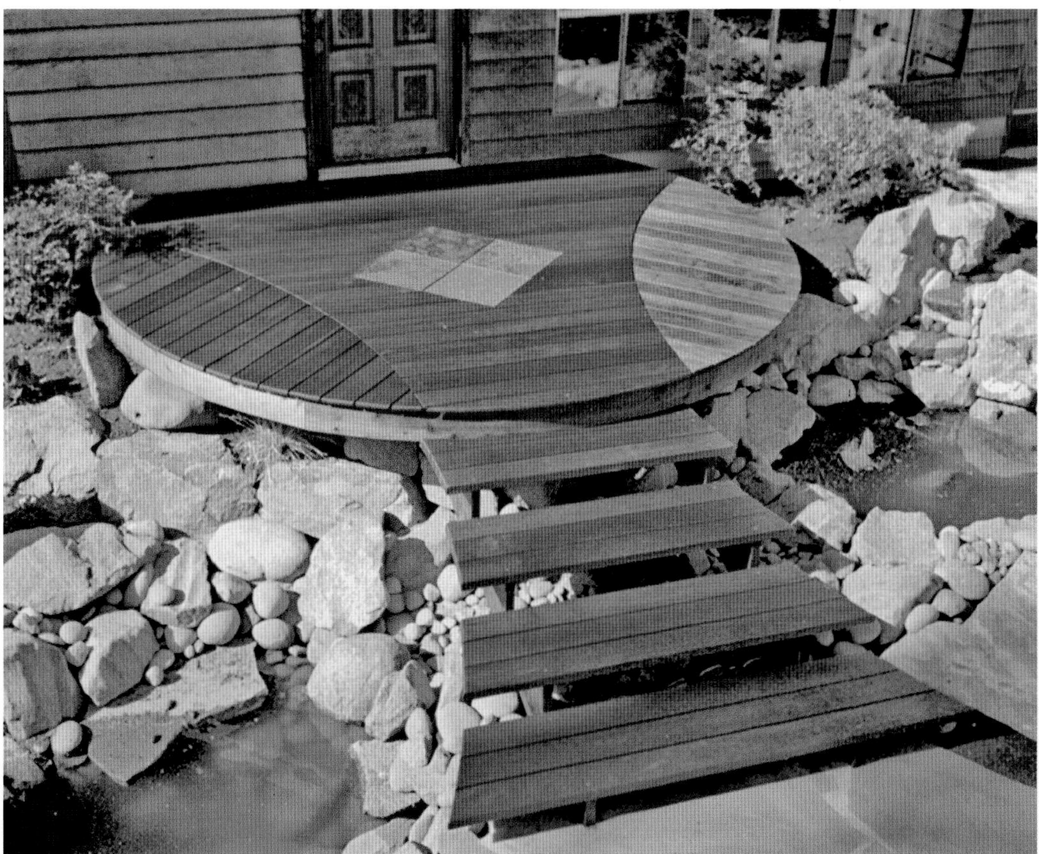

Look beyond obvious spaces for deck opportunities. This entryway is well-served by a tiny deck that is part of a sophisticated entrance design. The curved shape is inviting and space-efficient, directing visitors up the stairs, over the rock moat, and right to the front door. The dark hue of the ipe hardwood decking reinforces the visual sense of a small, intimate landing space in front of the door.

Don't let small equal dull. This deck, nestled into the inside corner of the house, features a three-tone color scheme and superb detailing including enclosed skirting. The combination makes the deck feel like it is an integral part of the sophisticated architecture. But the landscaping is what provides a finished look to the installation. Foundation plantings and groomed beds help make a small deck blend seamlessly with the house at large.

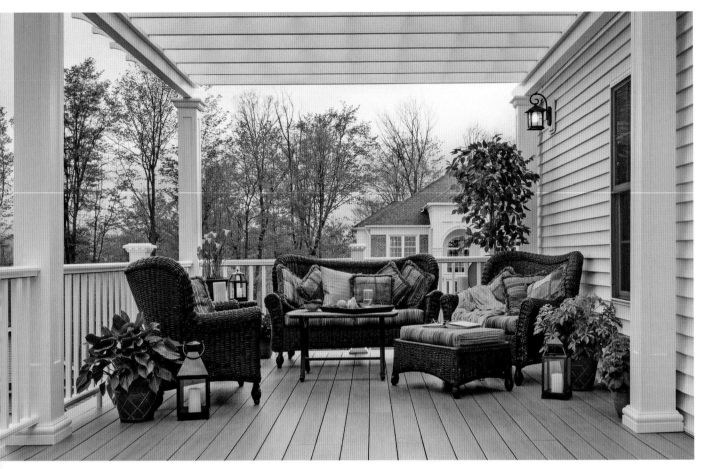

Cultivate "cozy" as a theme for a small deck. Although the natural inclination for a small deck may be to underfurnish it in an effort to make it seem larger, the more effective strategy is to crowd the space with a thoughtful configuration of comfortable yet stylish outdoor furnishings. Small touches, like the candle lanterns here, make for a warm space that invites nesting and small-group socializing.

Use a small deck to complement a traditional covered porch. This deck, designed with an interesting shape and decking that matches the porch alongside, serves as an ideal open platform from which to sunbathe or enjoy a star-filled night sky. Railing and stair lights make it safe and comfortable after dark and ensure that it's usable for warm-night cocktails.

Small Decks

Use deck shape and size to set the mood of an outdoor space. This simple, square deck fits perfectly into the corner of the house, but also suits the style of the space. The modest deck complements the restrained dimensions, and the offset step adds visual interest. Stepping stones, a linear border, and Japanese-influenced privacy fence all reinforce the notion of a peaceful Zen garden, with the gray composite deck functioning as a meditative platform.

Keep small decks interesting with intriguing shapes and luxury features. This tiny outdoor dining area is just large enough to accommodate a small table and chairs for warm-weather cookouts. The money saved from building such a modest construction allows for details not found on many decks. A built-in bench adds seating and style, while built-in planters offer beautiful seasonal accents.

Go vertical on a small deck to increase excitement. This tiny deck was built of stunning ipe hardwood in deep reddish browns. But as lovely as the wood itself is, the details are even more impressive. Built-in benches and planters ensure this is one very comfortable outdoor room. The elaborate designs of the railings and overhang supports add to the feeling of a cozy, welcoming space, perfect for reading the paper or having a drink with a few close friends.

Design a dedicated dining area on a small deck. With limited space to exploit, it's always a wise idea to focus a tiny deck on a single purpose. One of the best uses for a small deck is a dining area, especially where the deck is placed off a back door leading to a kitchen or indoor dining area. A few bold accents, like the bright red chairs in this ensemble, make for a vibrant look that is way bigger than the space would indicate.

Small Decks

Exploit the view from a slope with a restrained deck. Small decks are ideal where the view is unrivaled but the location would present construction nightmares for a larger structure. A small deck like this one is just enough to sit and enjoy the watery scene from the back of the house. The gray-and-white color scheme makes for a smart, clean addition to the house, and an uncomplicated design keeps costs in line.

Build a small deck in an unconventional shape for maximum bang for your buck. Shaped like an octagon, this deck features both usable floor space and an intriguing footprint sure to draw interest from any backyard visitor. The deck was crafted of beautiful redwood; small decks are ideal opportunities to use high-end materials in your outdoor surfaces without breaking the bank.

Allow for pathways of natural transition from inside to out, on small decks. This deck includes a very comfortable sitting area, from which the homeowners can enjoy the lovely outdoor setting. But the path from backdoor to backyard is left clear, providing both visual and physical flow. The wide stairs makes this an accessible—and more usable—structure.

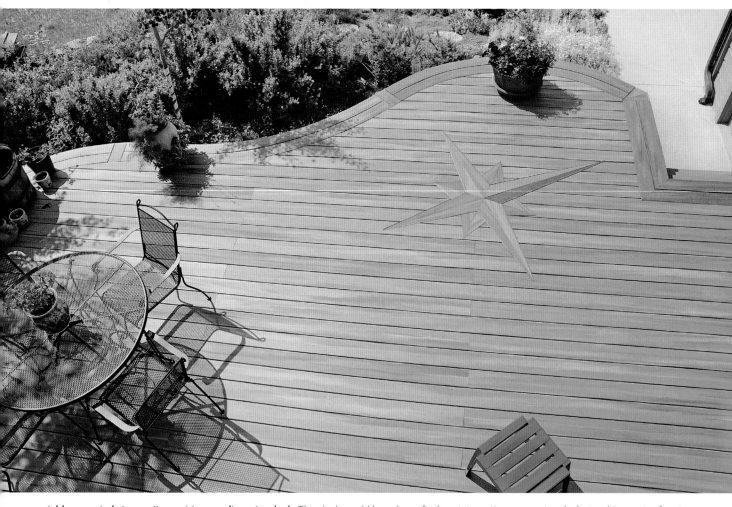

Add curves to bring excitement to a medium-size deck. This deck would have been fairly uninteresting as a rectangle, but a chic curving front creates the contour of a grand piano. The shape blends the edge of the deck nicely with the yard's profuse flowering shrubs. The inlaid compass star completes a deck design that, while simple, is incredibly stylish.

Craft a midsize deck of composites for construction flexibility and special features. This outdoor living room is stylized with a diamond inlay in contrasting color to the field decking and with boards running in four different directions. The composite material makes creating the inlay easy. It is also simple to build in seductive curves such as those that define the front edge of the deck.

Medium Decks

Avoid "bowling alley syndrome." The builder of this long, narrow rectangular deck circumvented that fate by creating a bump-out that serves as a comfortable alcove for seating and creates a more dynamic shape for the deck. Making the deck even more unusual, the long inner side has been left unattached to the house, with a bench serving as both railing and additional seating.

Make a midsize deck majestic with hardwood. As this example plainly illustrates, build a highly detailed hardwood deck with two levels and a dynamic shape and you create a showstopper. This deck includes well-designed railings with double top rails and benches and planters crafted of the same stunning wood. Add in a few light posts and decorative fixtures, and the result is a structure that is so beautiful on its own that it seems like a shame to add any furniture.

COMPUTER-AIDED DECK DESIGN

Looking for a dynamite deck design? Put down your sketchpad and pencil, and turn to the computer. You can find a wealth of computer-aided design (CAD) programs specifically created to help the homeowner design the ideal deck. Derived from powerful, complex CAD software used by professionals such as architects, the deck design programs available today are user-friendly, adaptable, and incredibly helpful. Most people will be able to master any of these programs within a couple hours. The software allows you to create a representation of your home, design the deck to highly detailed specifications, and see your creation in a color, three-dimensional model. Although you are likely to find the ability to preview potential designs one of the most attractive features, these programs also provide other useful functions, such as materials calculators, the ability to swap elements with a few clicks of the mouse, and ways to keep track of costs once you start your project.

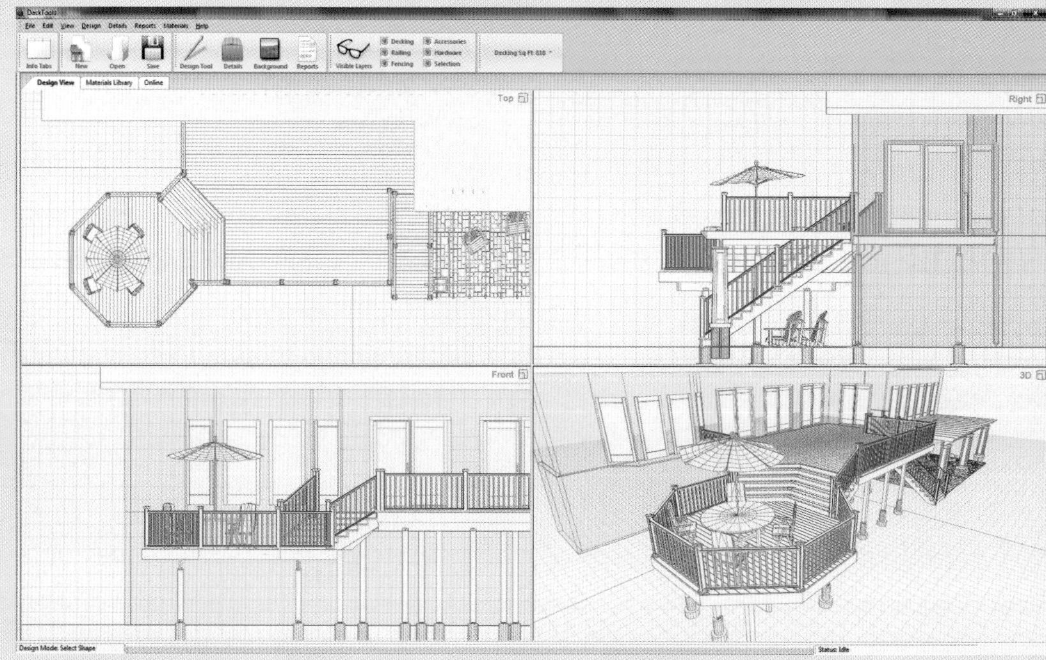

Many deck design programs allow you to create plan views—elevation drawings detailed enough to be accepted by some building departments as part of the permit process. These elevation plans can be extremely helpful if you are hiring a contractor or deck builder to construct the deck for you.

This screen capture is representative of the level of detail you can expect from most deck-design programs. The software creates scale models of the deck you've designed, and many programs allow you to view the deck from multiple angles. You can also change the color of the deck to see how it would look crafted from different decking materials.

Isolate sections to give the impression of even more spaciousness. This lovely, well-designed deck unfolds from the intimate dining area that has been placed right outside the home's kitchen, to more general seating areas that would be appropriate for a party. A separate fire pit area has been designed as part of—but apart from—the deck at large, allowing for nighttime stargazing or fireside cocktails.

Use curves to carve a midsize deck out of an unusual yard shape. Rather than build the deck out into the landscape (and face the construction challenges that might entail), the designer of this deck used PVC decking to create a fabulous curved surface that is almost poetic in its appearance. The curved shape leaves plenty of room for different activity areas, and the theme is carried through with curving boards that cut through the field decking.

Let a large deck sprawl. The inclination with a large deck is often to go multilevel. But straightforward is sometimes better, especially when you have the acreage around your home. This deck is built with an open floor plan, and accented with extremely high-end furniture including an outdoor sofa, as well as built-in features such as a sideboard in the dining area and planters where the deck receives the most sun. Crisp white rails perfectly complement the light synthetic decking.

Create a very pleasing look by using symmetry to provide visual balance. This attractive deck includes matching border benches on either side that not only offer abundant seating, they also help focus the eye and lead the visitor to the stone path running out into the backyard. The homeowner has carried through the idea of symmetry with planters on either side the sliding glass doors.

Be extravagant where space is not an issue—such as in this acre-size backyard. This deck features several outdoor "rooms," with a large spa tub, a separate fireplace seating area, and cooking and dining sections. The abundance of space allows each area enough separation to stand on its own, with the decking tying all of them together.

DECK PERSPECTIVES

Every deck must take into account several different points of view. The most obvious is the perspective from the deck looking out into the yard and surroundings. But the deck also changes the view from inside the house, altering the perspective the homeowner sees as he or she looks out a window or through glass doors. No less important, the deck will greatly affect the appearance of the house.

All of these are most affected by the level of the deck. A ground-level platform is less likely to dramatically change the view from inside the house, and it will usually only have a modest impact on how the house's architecture is perceived. A multilevel or elevated deck will provide a much greater vista of the yard and beyond, while also radically changing how the architecture is perceived. Obviously, how you site your deck is an extremely important part of your design.

But beyond view and appearances, the levels of your deck are also a structural concern. It will always be easier to build a deck at ground level on a nice, flat, level plot. The higher and more complicated the deck is, the greater the engineering must be to ensure that it is safe. Structural reinforcement also adds to the cost of the project. That's why, ultimately, the final perspective of any deck design is a balance between the look—or looks—you desire and the more fundamental, practical concerns of construction.

Add variation for excitement. Although this deck is built at ground level, it includes a step-up level of its own, providing visual diversity and a seating area separate from the main stage of the deck. Bushy flowering perennials and low-growing evergreen shrubs help blend the structure into the surrounding yard.

Help a deck look crisp by using fascia boards around the perimeter. The fascia on this deck matches the composite decking material used on top—replicating the coloring and patterns of ipe hardwood. Matching fascia boards create the illusion of a solid box set level on the ground. Separate dining, fire pit, and spa tub areas are defined simply by furniture placement, rather than separate platform levels.

Simplify your deck by foregoing a foundation. Done right, as in the case of this small backyard deck, even a tiny deck can make a big impact on the yard and house. The designer of this composite deck chose a bold treatment, with darker border boards, decking installed on a diagonal, and a bridge that crosses a rock pond. The effect is far more eye-catching than the square footage would suggest.

Separate a ground-level deck from the house, in situations where an attached deck would be out of place. The rear of this home is situated so low that it is almost sunken into the surrounding terrain. A deck—even on ground level—would not have lined up with doors and windows. Building the deck in the middle of the yard ensures that the structure doesn't disrupt the look of architecture and makes the most of sun exposure. The surface is ideal for soaking up the rays.

Ground-Level Decks

Answer the homeowner's needs first. This composite ground-level deck was designed and built to blend in seamlessly without calling much attention to itself. The solid-color deck material seems almost like an extension of the home's painted walls, and the triple steps leading from twin sets of sliding glass doors make a seamless visual connection from inside to out.

Increase the visual impact of a ground-level deck with an unusual orientation. This stunning hardwood deck is made even more so through an uncommon, angular design. Rather than raise the deck to the house level, the builder used a set of steps to a transition platform at the back door. The deck is integrated with the yard through strategically placed plantings, and a bit of flair is added with a wing shaped sail over the sitting area.

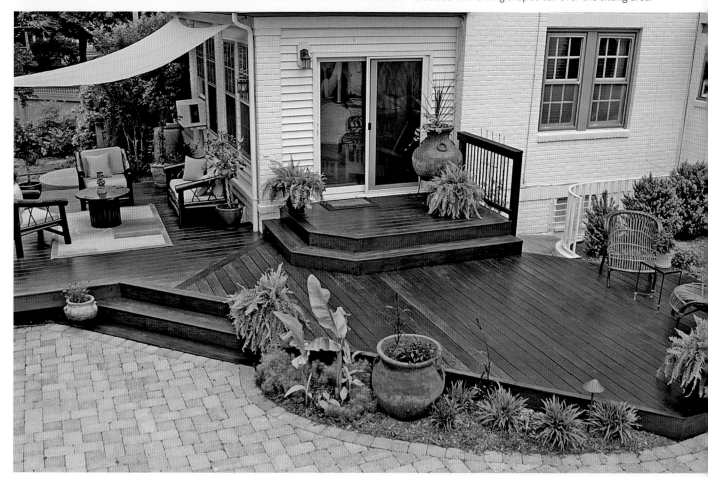

Match the size of an elevated deck to the location. This gently curved, very slightly elevated front entryway deck provides much of the charm of a porch, without overwhelming the front yard or walk leading up to the door. By elevating the deck a bit above ground level, the designer makes it appear more like an attractive, inviting extension of the entryway threshold.

Integrate a deck by elevating it. Although this deck could have been built in levels stepped down the slope behind the house, the feeling is much more bucolic and ethereal by projecting the surface into the trees. The feeling of is one of seclusion, privacy and calm. The perfect atmosphere to enjoy a soak in a spa tub . . . while enjoying a few seasonal decorations!

Elevated Decks

Enjoy the sun and any view more by elevating a deck. A bright white aluminum railing adds style to a deck that doubles as a sunbathing platform during the day and a social center any time. The structure was positioned to take advantage of a scenic stand of trees surrounding the yard, which would have bathed a lower deck in shade.

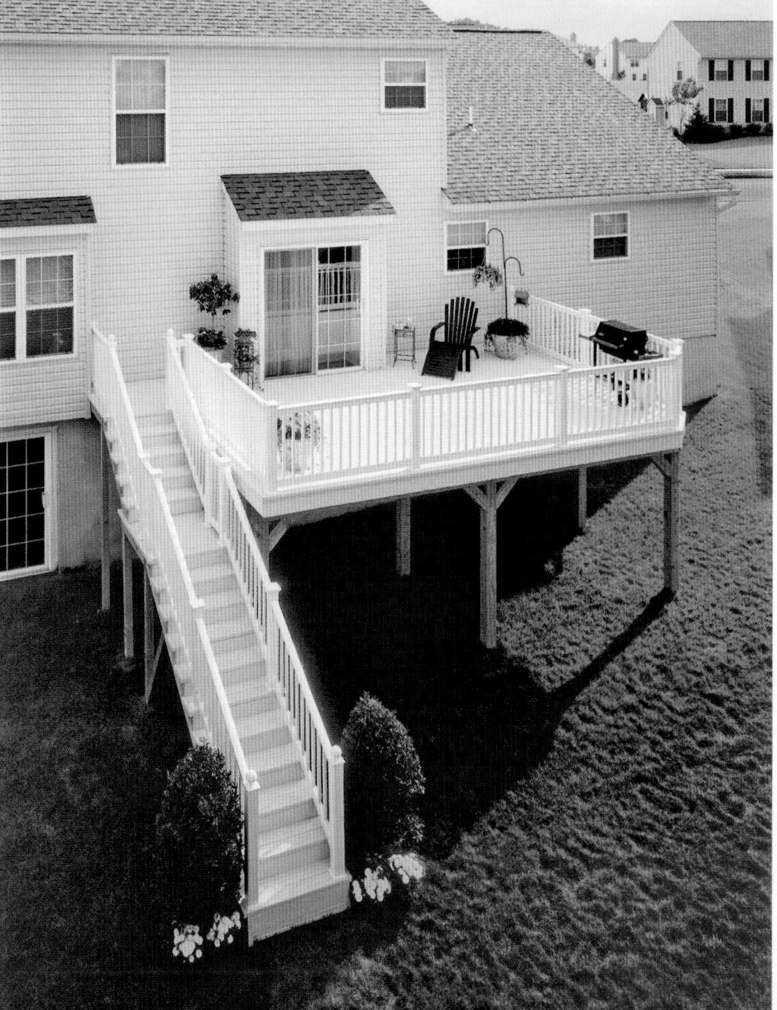

Solve the problem of a sloped site. This house featured a grass-covered backyard that was pleasant to look at but too steep to use for summer cookouts or entertaining. The second-floor deck serves those purposes nicely and provides an excellent vantage point for looking out over the peaceful view. The supports for the deck were left exposed because they'll rarely be viewed from the seldom-used yard.

Choose from a variety of options to deal with less-than-attractive supporting framework. Although you can landscape around the deck, the option here is one of the best: cladding the outside of the foundation with skirting of the same material as the deck surface. The wide composite fascia and skirting used on this deck matches the deck and stairs, creating a unified design that makes for an attractive platform, especially when lit at night.

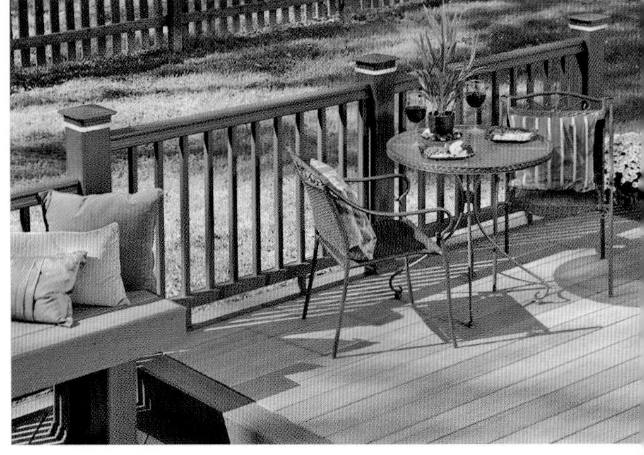

Add a rail for definition and safety. Although a deck like this one may not be required by code to have a railing, adding one increases the sense of a platform independent from the yard itself. It creates visual separation and, more importantly, stops anyone from stepping off the side. A step off even a low deck can be jarring. Of course adding a railing also presents a vast number of decorative options.

Elegantly conceal a support structure with wraparound stairs. The stairs on this simple deck are crafted of the same wood as the deck itself, which makes the entire structure visually read like one solid piece. Wraparound stairs are a lot of work to design and install, but the final appearance is usually well worth the effort.

Add a powerful design element with a curved façade. This hardwood deck emphasizes the prow of the structure with a contrasting white fascia that makes the deck visually project out even more. Decorative railings and lattice between the stained supports below the deck create an interesting cantilevered look.

Use two simple levels for different entrances. This handsome ipe deck actually has a fairly simple form, with full-length steps marking each level. The cookout and dining area has been placed on the upper level, just outside of French doors leading to the dining room. The lower level is attached to the doors leading to the living room. This construction allows for a maximum of access and ease of use any time.

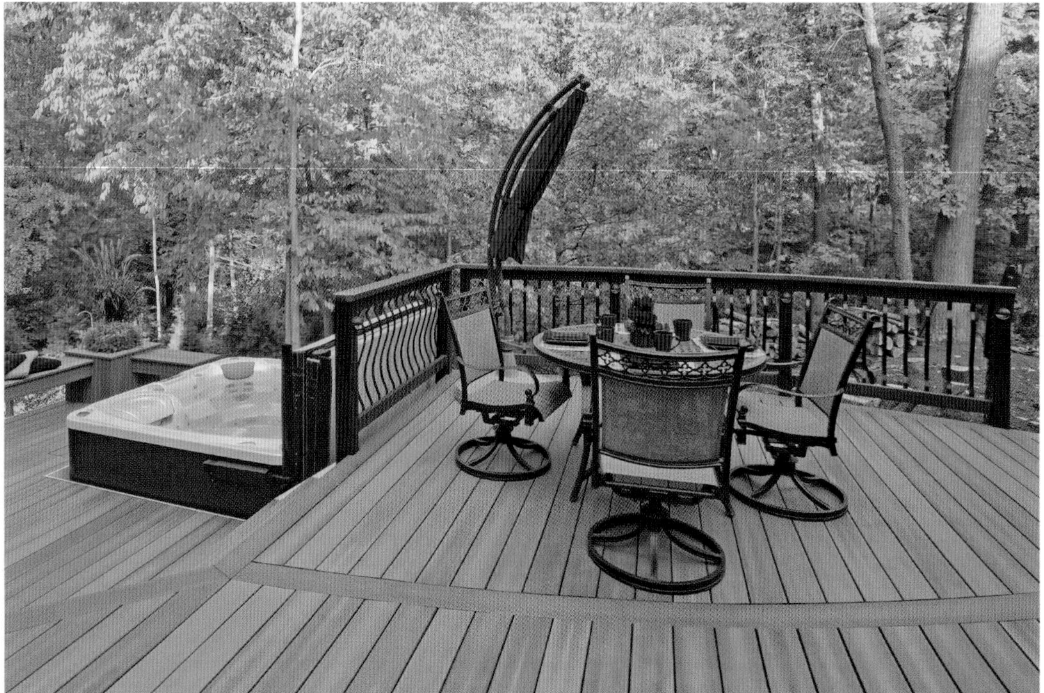

Spa tubs go on lower levels. Although this may seem counterintuitive (it can be a long wet trek back into the house), there are good reasons for the rule. A lower placement means that the tub is kept away from the dining area, with food, drink, and glassware that doesn't belong around a tub. The location also makes sure it's easier to reinforce and support the weight of the tub.

Multilevel Decks

Exploit the potential in large decks to show off big style. This fabulous deck features cascading levels that flow into one another by way of elegantly curved steps. Built-in planters help define the different levels, and a spa tub serves as a visual centerpiece of the two-tone composite surface. A sizable inlaid compass rose adds even more polish to an already sophisticated look.

Institute an amazingly clean look by using all-white decking and railings. Even the enclosed pergola roof is white on this showcase structure. Cladding a pergola in a solid surface helps block the direct sun for cool meals on hot days, and means the space can be used even in inclement weather. Post-cap lights are as practical as they are pretty, making the deck usable during the night as well as the day.

DECKS IN THE LANDSCAPE

The best decks just look like they belong. They seem right in proportion to the house, and they complement rather than compete with the landscape. One of the best ways to make your deck look like it's always been there is by creating tangible connections between the structure itself and your landscape.

That isn't really hard to do, if you consider the layout of your yard when designing your deck. A strong link between the structure you build and the property you own can actually be established in a number of different ways—or a combination of them. You can, for example, shape a deck to conform to hallmark features in the landscape. Many deck designers do this by including access holes for beautiful old trees to grow right through the surface of the deck. You can also carry through the theme of a garden or landscape by decorating the deck with planters potted with similar plants. Of course, a natural way to integrate the deck into a yard is to landscape around the structure once you've completed it.

Whatever technique you use, always keep in mind the view from the deck—yet another excellent way to reinforce the connection with natural surroundings. Position your deck to look over foliage and flowers from three sides, and you create an immediate link to that vegetation. A scene thick with plant life creates a wonderful mood, conducive to relaxation, easy socializing and, ultimately, complete enjoyment of the space. Successfully make the connection between nature and your deck and you'll create a structure that not only serves as a perfect transition from inside to out, but one that improves both yard and garden.

Consider any overgrown landscaping a potential design tool in your deck design. As this deck illustrates, positioning the deck so that flowering and evergreen shrubs invade the borders of the deck is a great way to blur the distinction between built structure and natural garden. This composite surface seems to disappear into plant life on every side, not only blending the deck, but also creating a dreamy environment for relaxing or eating outside.

Decks in the Landscape

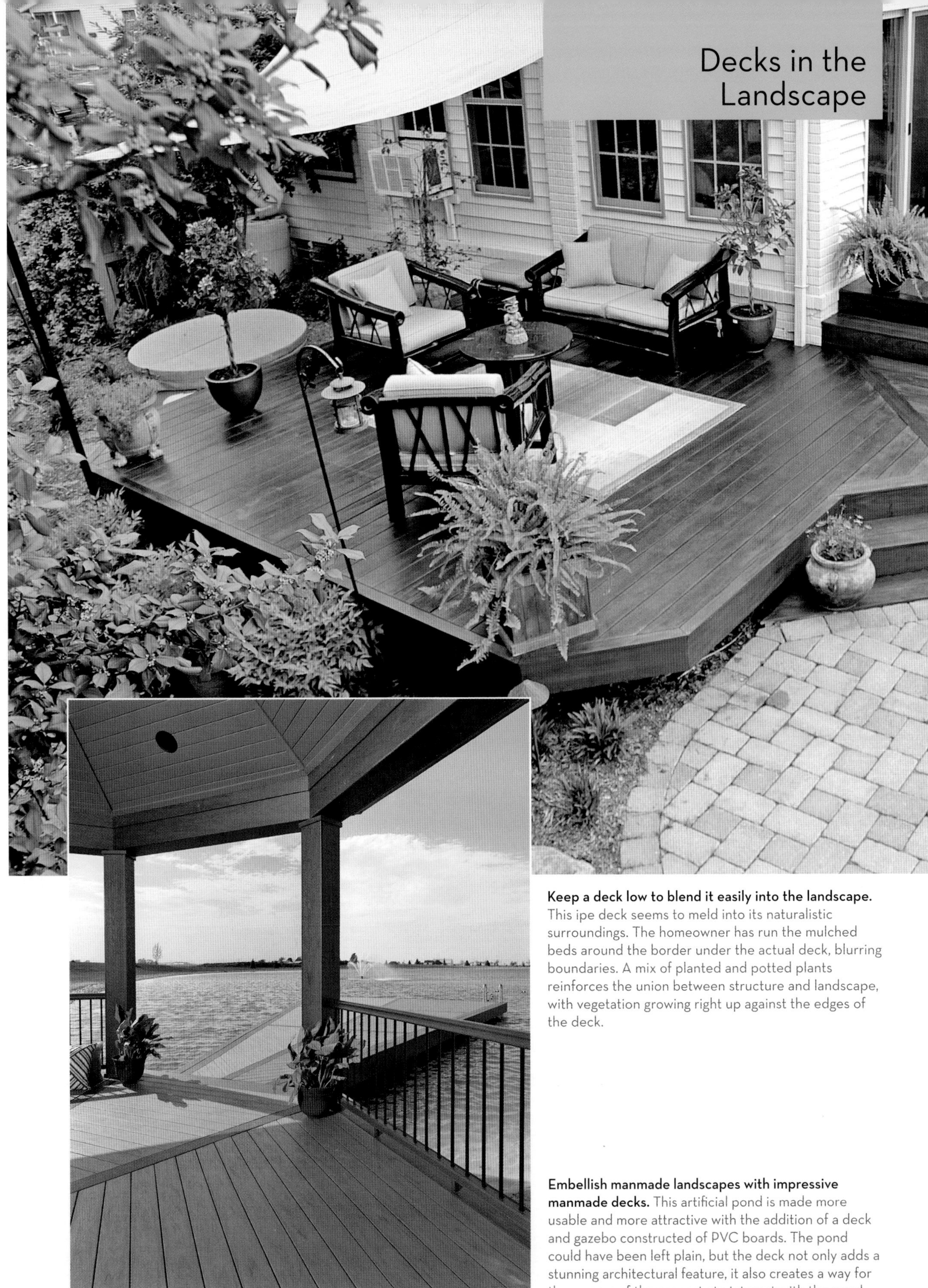

Keep a deck low to blend it easily into the landscape. This ipe deck seems to meld into its naturalistic surroundings. The homeowner has run the mulched beds around the border under the actual deck, blurring boundaries. A mix of planted and potted plants reinforces the union between structure and landscape, with vegetation growing right up against the edges of the deck.

Embellish manmade landscapes with impressive manmade decks. This artificial pond is made more usable and more attractive with the addition of a deck and gazebo constructed of PVC boards. The pond could have been left plain, but the deck not only adds a stunning architectural feature, it also creates a way for the owners of the property to interact with the pond.

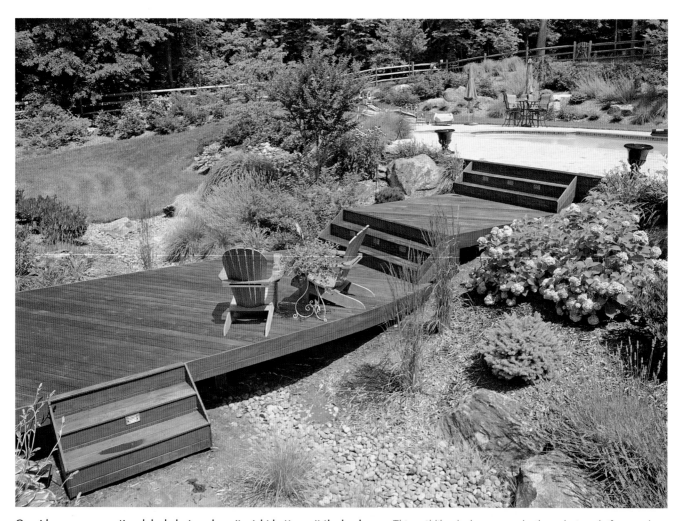

Consider an unconventional deck design where it might better suit the landscape. This pathlike deck serves as both a relaxing platform and a walkway from the house to the pool. The levels of the deck follow the contours of the yard, and run the structure right through informal plantings. The placement means that sunbathers relax in the midst of the landscape.

Reverse the traditional relationship. This homeowner created a garden bed under the deck's wood staircase. The color and form of the ornamental grasses and informal scattering of low-growing shrubs perfectly complement the rustic look of the wood rails and stairs. The result is a staircase that visually roots the deck into the landscape.

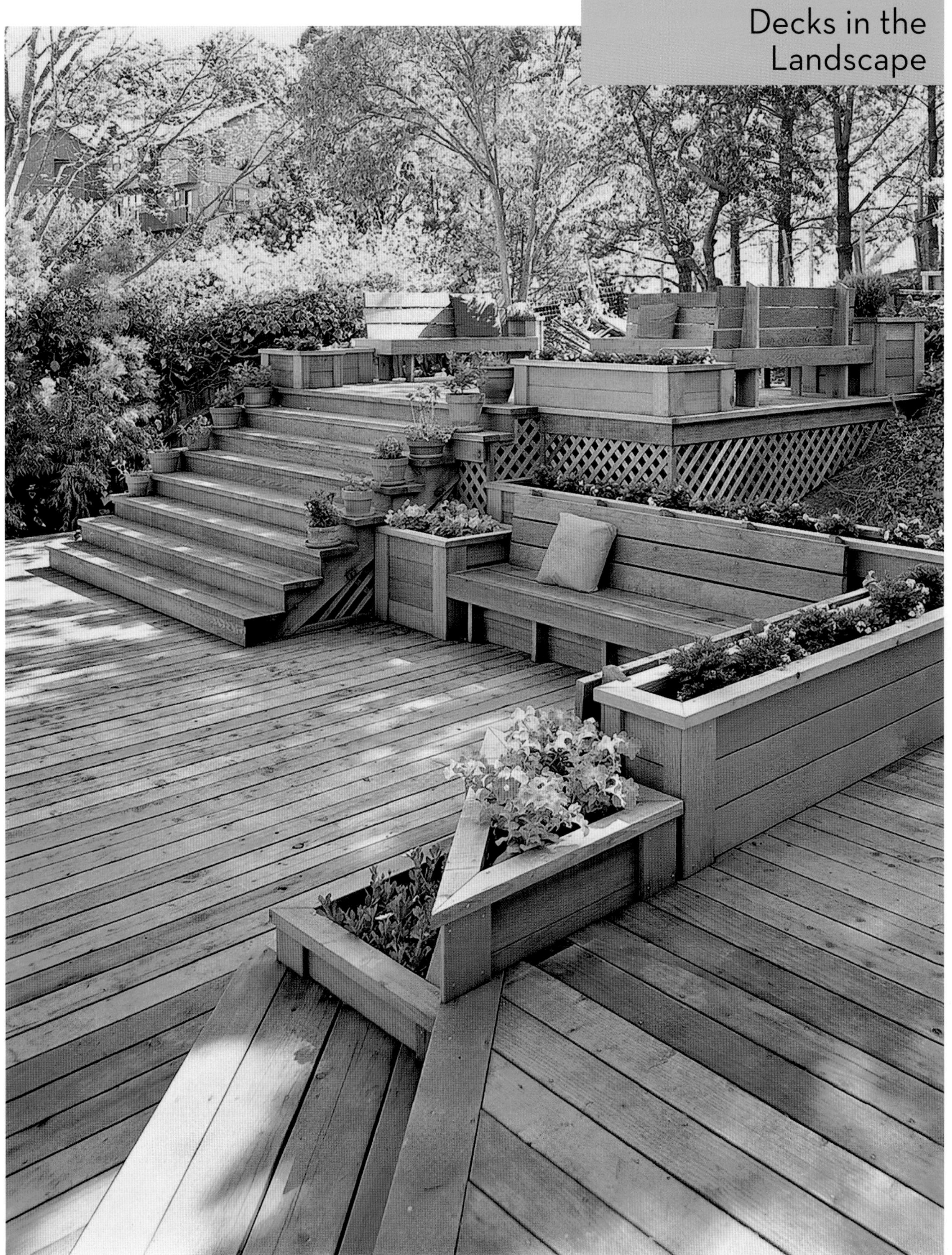

Merge the deck with the landscape by hugging the existing topography. This is an especially effective strategy when dealing with multiple levels, as with this deck. The multilevel design was arranged to almost organically nestle into the hillside, effectively making it look like it has been there forever and is just an extension of the landscape. The use of redwood decking reinforces this perception, because the wood's color blends so well with plants and soil.

Extend the home's floorspace into dense natural surroundings. This expansive deck was designed with a seemingly random outdoor border that follows the contours of the wooded hillside behind the house. The deck has been built with an opening to allow a tree to grow through the surface, and further tie the outdoor space to the surrounding environment.

Make the most of any woodsy setting. This basic wood platform was built on a large wooded property, but rather than cut down trees to make room for a larger deck, the deck was designed to jut out into a copse of trees. The tree canopies hang over the deck, creating a very bucolic feel and cool shade for hot summer days.

Decks in the Landscape

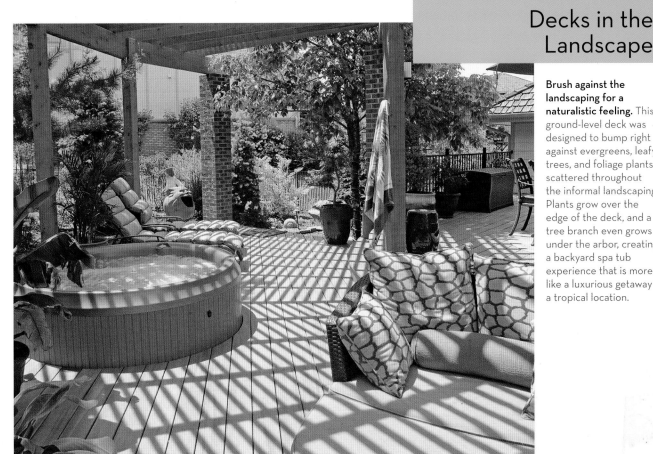

Brush against the landscaping for a naturalistic feeling. This ground-level deck was designed to bump right up against evergreens, leafy trees, and foliage plants scattered throughout the informal landscaping. Plants grow over the edge of the deck, and a tree branch even grows under the arbor, creating a backyard spa tub experience that is more like a luxurious getaway in a tropical location.

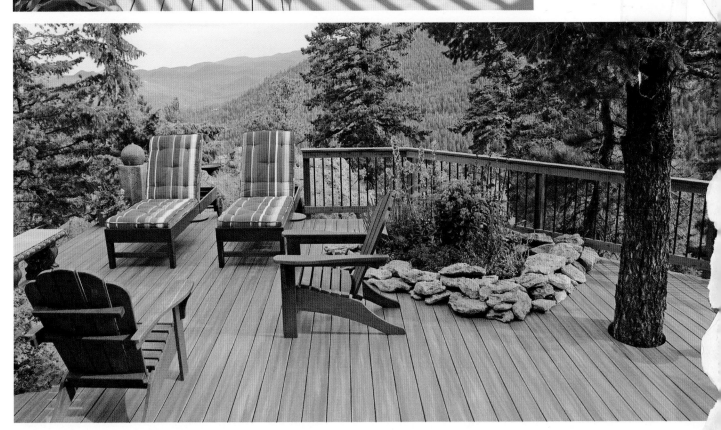

Make room for an old-growth tree right in the middle of a deck. A stunning mountainside deck benefits from a unique design that accommodates a tree inside a "tree ring" built into the deck's surface. Tree rings are simple to integrate for experienced deck builders. They are a way for the deck to coexist with large, older trees. This homeowner went one step further and added a self-contained deck-top garden with a plastic liner and rock walls.

FOCUS ON PURPOSE

Make installing a deck spa tub easy by building around a ground-level footing. This deck was built with a stepped cutout that embraces the spa tub, making it appear to be built into the deck. In reality, the tub sits on a footing that is smartly colored to match the decking. The tub is centrally located and accessible from all parts of the deck, so it easy to include bathers in party conversation.

The best decks are the most usable decks. The most usable decks are those that are designed to accommodate whatever the homeowner wants to do on the deck. A deck built just to fill space or without any thought to how it will be used is a waste of money, time, and effort.

The purpose of the deck should be foremost in the homeowner's mind right from the start. The specific use should drive deck design and planning, because different features will require vastly different construction. A built-in outdoor kitchen will need power or gas run to the grill. A spa tub will require additional reinforcement and plumbing. If you're hoping to use the deck for multiple purposes, you'll probably need different levels linked by stairs or transition platforms.

Regardless, the options are vast. Most homeowners like to include at least a dining area, if not a full-blown dry bar and prep area for cookouts. A fully equipped outdoor kitchen is a huge undertaking, but if you live in a warm area of the country and spend three seasons living outside, it can be a worthwhile investment. If you're a water lover, a spa tub may be the ideal focal point for your backyard deck, especially if it's installed to complement an existing pool. Of course, you can opt for simpler construction and lower expense if all you're looking for from your deck is a quiet, comfortable place to look out over natural surroundings or stargaze at night. Whatever it might be, keep the ultimate use in mind and you'll never regret the deck you build.

Relaxing in a Tub

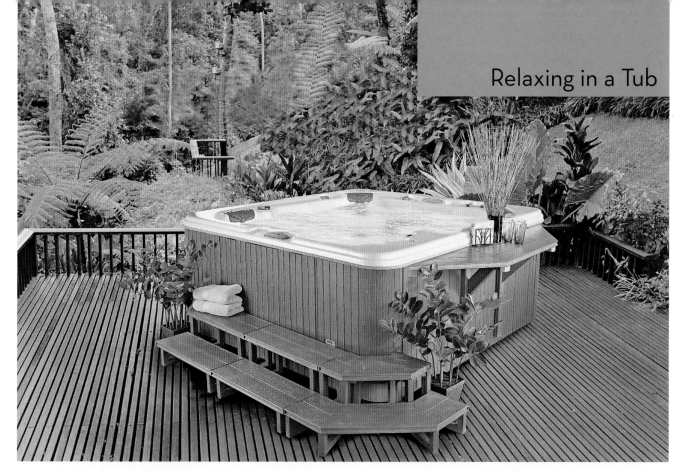

Marry spa tubs to tropical settings for a dynamic look and feel. The owner of this deck and tub has nestled the feature into a landscape that might as well be an island paradise. The slat decking and low railing provide an understated foil that allows the tub and surroundings to dominate the scene. The tubside ledge adds a little useful luxury to the picture, providing a handy place for drinks and food.

Make your spa tub a centerpiece. Here, the round deck is meant merely as a stage for the tub, isolated in the center of a patio. When planning a tub deck location, keep the view in mind as the owner of this tub did; the feature's positioning takes advantage of the rural setting's wonderful 360-degree view. Because no neighbors are within sight, privacy is not an issue.

Turn to tradition to make an entertaining mecca. Although jetted spa tubs have come to dominate the market, an old-fashioned wood hot tub still holds its charms. These features are ideal as the centerpiece for a party deck, including a bar, casual sitting area, and fun decorative features like the metal art behind this tub.

Define the spa tub area to make it special. A pergola and matching privacy screen help separate the spa tub on this deck. Privacy screens are elegant ways to create intimate spaces for tubbing out of view of neighbors or even other people in the house. The pergola breaks up direct sun but still allows a view of the stars for enjoying the tub at night.

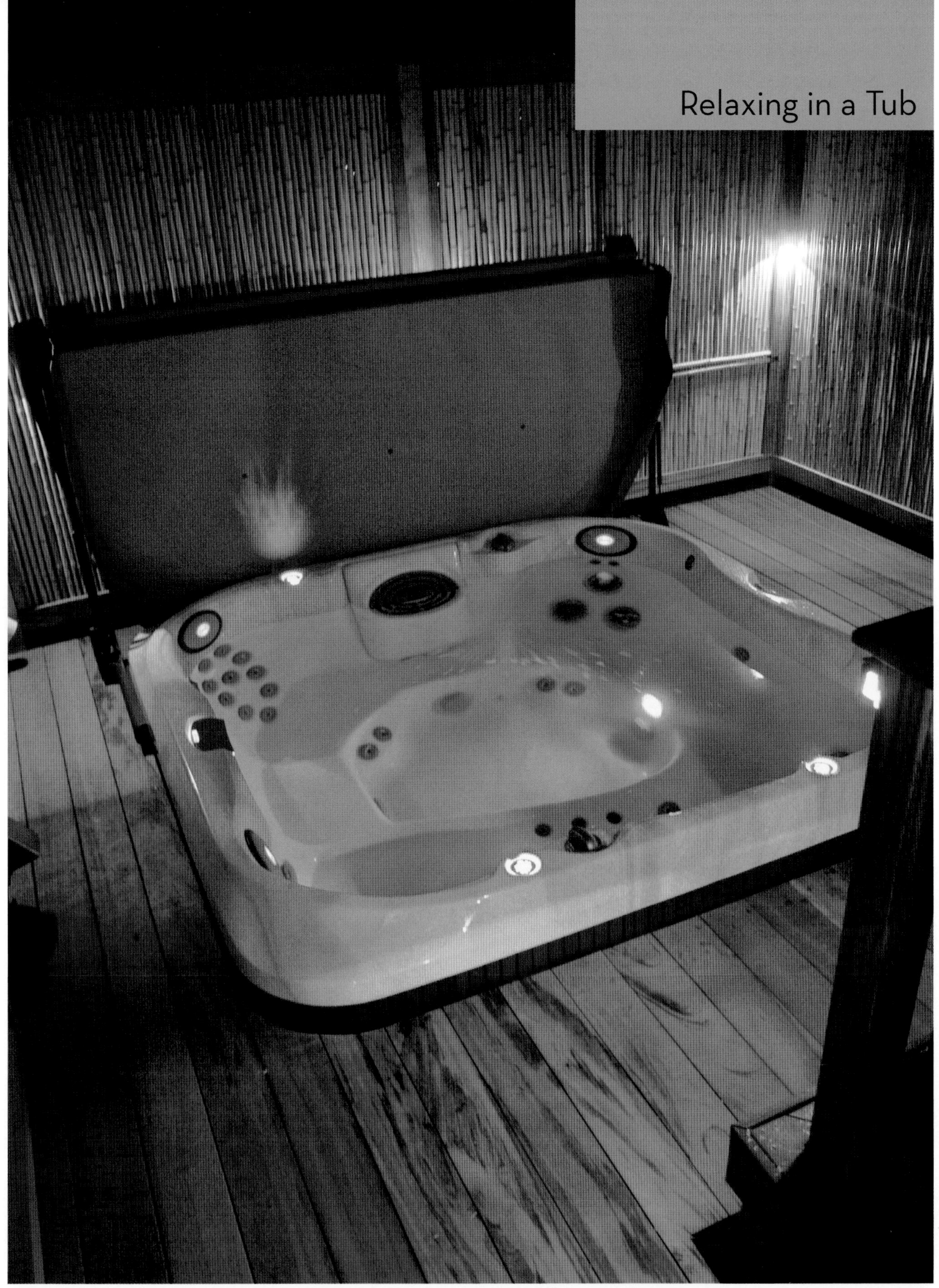

Relaxing in a Tub

Create a secluded spa heaven when you have a luxurious, high-end spa tub to showcase. The deck here was crafted of tigerwood that is, like many other hardwoods, resistant to mold, water damage, cracking, and slipping. The appearance of the deck is stunning, but no less so at night, when the tub's lavender lights illuminate the heated water to create a nearly surreal vision of relaxation. Consider colored lighting to spruce up the look of a basic tub or pool.

Allow a tub enclosure to dominate a smaller deck. These homeowners use their spa tub as the centerpiece of outdoor parties. The deck layout facilitates easy access to the spa tub itself, and keeps adjacent seating close enough for bathers and nonbathers to pleasantly interact. The deck's clear, heart-grade redwood has been sealed but is naturally resistant to rot, wear, and cracking.

Consider accents that will increase the usability and enjoyment of a deck-bound spa tub. Here, the owner has opted to supplement the tub with steps, planters, and bleacher seating, all supplied by the tub's manufacturer. Notice that the tub's surround matches the composite decking. Many manufacturers offer a choice of tub surrounds to help the feature blend in with the decking you've selected.

Relaxing in a Tub

Opt for a spa tub for any multilevel deck. This hillside deck incorporates the tub into the second of three levels. The design makes both a natural progression on the steep slope, and separates the tub into its own space. Notice that the tub is accompanied by a built-in bench; built-in seating gives bathers a place to cool off or change into and out of bathing gear.

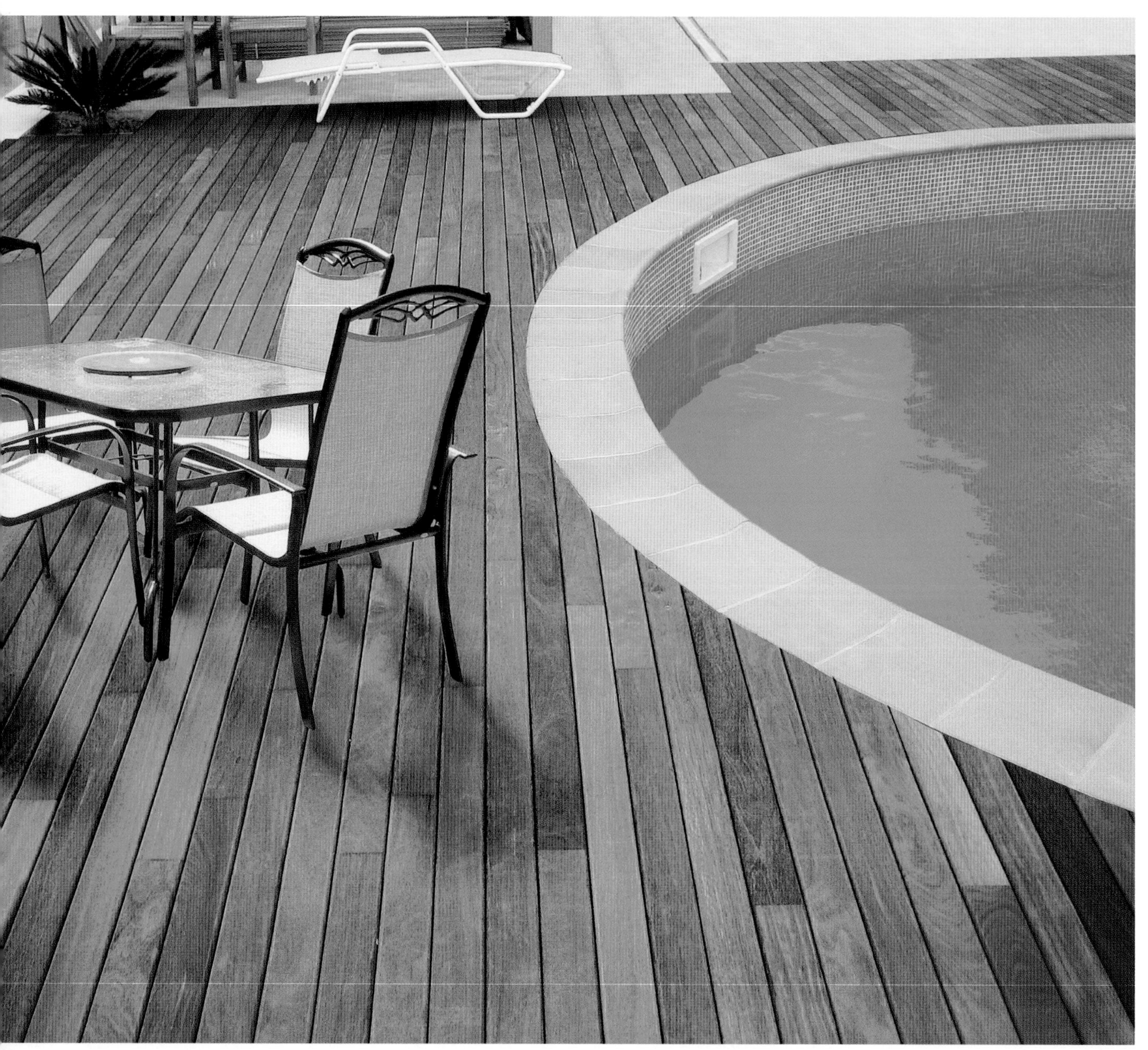

Match high-end decking to an in-ground pool. The luxury of a built-in pool calls for equally luxurious decking. This inviting oval pool with its simple formed lip is well served by a handsome cumaru hardwood deck. One of the densest hardwoods used for decking, cumaru is naturally resistant to insects, mold, rot, and water penetration. Installed around a pool, only the cut ends need to be water sealed.

Pool Fun

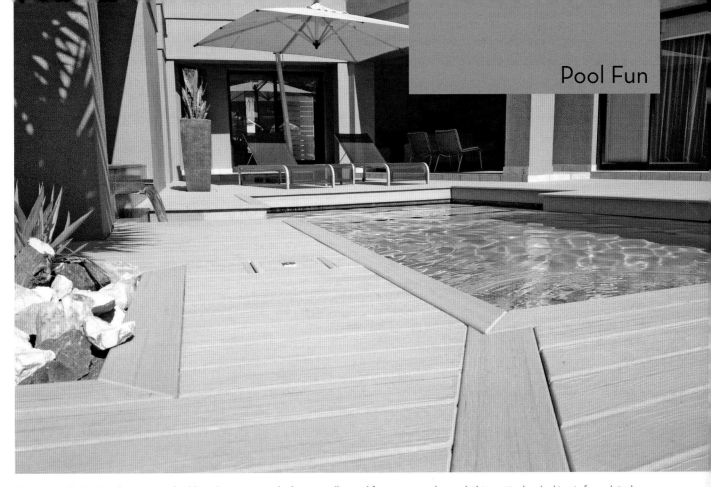

Pick the right decking for your pool. Although composite decking is well suited for use around a pool, this particular decking is formulated specifically for wet conditions and is almost completely resistant to any kind of moisture damage or mold growth. An added benefit is the textured top surface of the boards, which mimics the irregular surface of wood and ensures against slipping.

Contrast the pool area with the decking. Contrast can be as powerful as complementary design when it comes to the visual excitement between a pool and surrounding surfaces. The deck shown here leads from the main floor of the house down to a pool surrounded by a concrete patio. The darkness of the hardwood cumaru decking pops against the water and lighter surfaces. It provides a transition from beige house siding to pool area, one that includes seating overlooking the pool.

Leverage simplicity to emphasize elegance. Although this deck doesn't shout with color or pattern, the beige composite material creates a sophisticated look in a surface that is water- and wear-resistant. The designer crafted a stylish lip by running the decking over the edge of the pool and cladding it with a fascia board. The effect is sleek, modern, and pleasing to the eye.

Create a naturalistic scene by using redwood. Redwood is classic material to use around pools because it weathers well, complements the look of water, and feels great underfoot. It is also naturally slip-resistant. Although this deck has been sealed and will need to be maintained over time, some owners allow their redwood surfaces to age into a lovely weathered gray.

Complement both architecture and pool surface when choosing decking. This elegant gray composite decking provides a lovely transition from the color of the house to the color of the pool's lip. The shape of the deck roughly echoes the shape of the pool but with intriguing variations and bump-outs around the perimeter. Note how the direction of the boards around the outside of the pool forms a separate border. Board direction is a great way to create this kind of emphasis on a signature feature.

Use your pool deck as a design bridge. They are great for couching the pool in the style and context of the house—especially when the house features distinctive architecture. This modern home is complemented by a simple weathered redwood pool deck that echoes the basic straight lines of the architecture, with boards running perpendicular to the length of the pool. It's a simple and graceful look that serves the purpose admirably.

Detach the pool deck from the pool. The deck here is separated from the pool by a paver patio, but it still provides a shaded overhang—an ideal spot for swimmers to take a cooling time-out from playing in the pool. A privacy fence alongside the deck allows for dining in swimsuits without being self-conscious.

Pool Fun

Design your pool deck to allow plenty of room for socializing. Any pool deck needs to offer ample space for swimmers to get in and out of the pool, and others to circulate around the water feature. This large deck answers the call on both points. Although it is largely functional, the owner has added a bit of style by using wooden handrails finished in a natural tone that pops against the gray of the deck.

Elevate a deck for ideal poolside placement. Elevated decks provide a vantage point for parents to supervise youngsters playing in the pool, and they increase visual interest from the pool. This deck brings some stylistic fireworks in the form of stone posts that work well with the tan decking and skirting. The posts add a stately element to both deck and pool, enriching the entire scene.

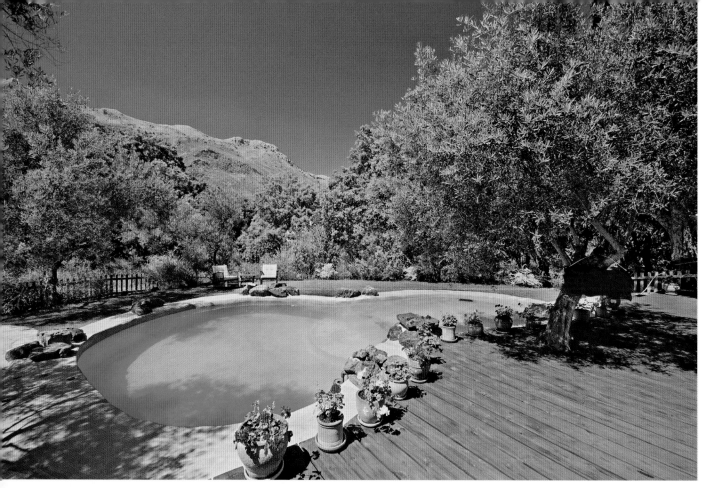

Follow the contour of the pool for the most effective deck design. Swimming pools are often distinctively shaped design elements, and the deck shape can help call attention to this hallmark feature. This kidney-shaped pool might have looked odd surrounded by a deck in a basic geometric shape. But the curving structure that was installed suits the pool well, with a row of potted plants to blur the boundary between weathered deck boards and the concrete pool edging.

Create dynamic tension. This wonderful redwood deck positions the pool as centerpiece, but it's the wood's distinctive color and grain that really tease the eye. A bump-out covered by a large pergola provides broken shade for swimmers who want to cool off, and a rail of the same wood provides a safety barrier required by most codes.

Pool Fun

Build function into a pool deck. This deck was constructed with steel rails for the domed pool cover. The pool cover slides along the rails to cover the pool in bad or cold weather, and swimmers can swim inside even when it's nasty outside. Notice the raised lid on the pool deck, which conceals the motor and controls for the pool cover. The lid blends fluidly with the rest of the deck, constructed of the same, water-resistant composite.

Design an infinity deck. Improve the look of an aboveground pool with a deck that butts right to the edge. As nice as they are to swim in, aboveground pools look less than sophisticated with the sides left exposed. A raised deck platform adds immeasurably to the appearance and provides very handy access to the water. Function and form are maximized in one structure.

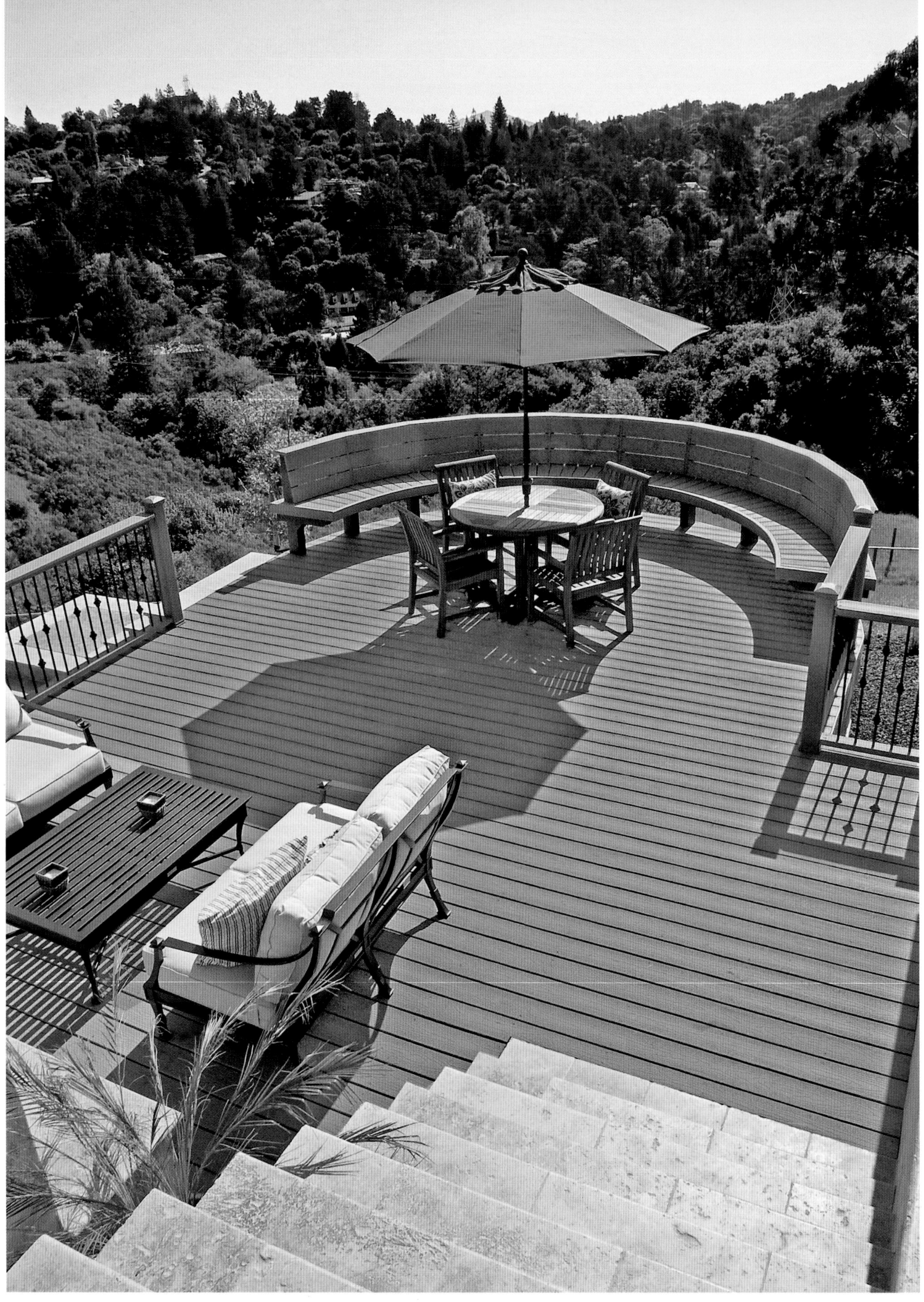

When you have a spectacular view, take advantage of it. This deck does just that, with a curving front edge like the prow of a ship. It projects out into the view, bringing the forested hillside almost within touching distance. The owner has provided two seating areas, one shaded and the other open to the sun. But thanks to the deck design, both enjoy a panoramic view of nature that is simply unrivaled.

Enjoying the View

Amplify the attraction of a stunning landscape feature. This slightly elevated composite deck includes a well-outfitted modern spa tub. The tub is placed where bathers can enjoy a tremendous woodsy view that will add to the enjoyment of the tub during any season. Built-in benches provide extra space for visitors who prefer to stay dry but still socialize.

Design to optimize a view. This second-floor deck is perfect for overlooking the treetops of the home's forested setting. Tempered-glass panels in the handrails ensure that as much of the view can be seen as possible. The benefit of a deck positioned this high is that the view of the night sky makes the deck just as nice during the evening.

Keep lighting and nighttime in mind. The deck after dark often provides a wholly different visual feast, sometimes even more intriguing than what you would see during the day. This multilevel deck has been lit with restraint, allowing hypnotic shadows to dominate the night landscape and barely illuminate the surface of the pool. The captivating scene is as nice a view as you'll find on any deck, day or night.

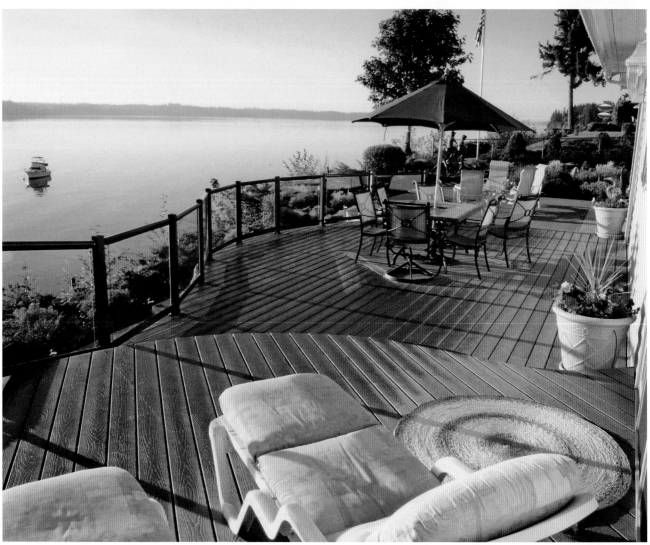

Don't waste a waterfront view. Any home along the shore of a body of water should have a majestic deck that follows the shoreline and transparent railings that allow for as much of the vista to shine through as possible. This view will be riveting in all types of weather and all seasons (a good reason for adding an outdoor heater or fire pit to a deck like this).

Enjoying the View

Position deck furniture to exploit wild flora. This large yard is filled with the plants of a forested landscape, one that provides almost endless fascination to anyone seated on the deck. Providing plenty of places to sit and an umbrella for shade—or to block the occasional raindrop—is smart and effective.

Create an impressive view while you take one in. If your home can accommodate one, a deck like this can be perfect for enjoying a gardener's gem or a well-landscaped yard. This deck was designed to project out over a professionally cultivated property complete with a rock garden and reflecting pool. The cabled handrails allow maximum view over the yard, and add big flair to the entire structure.

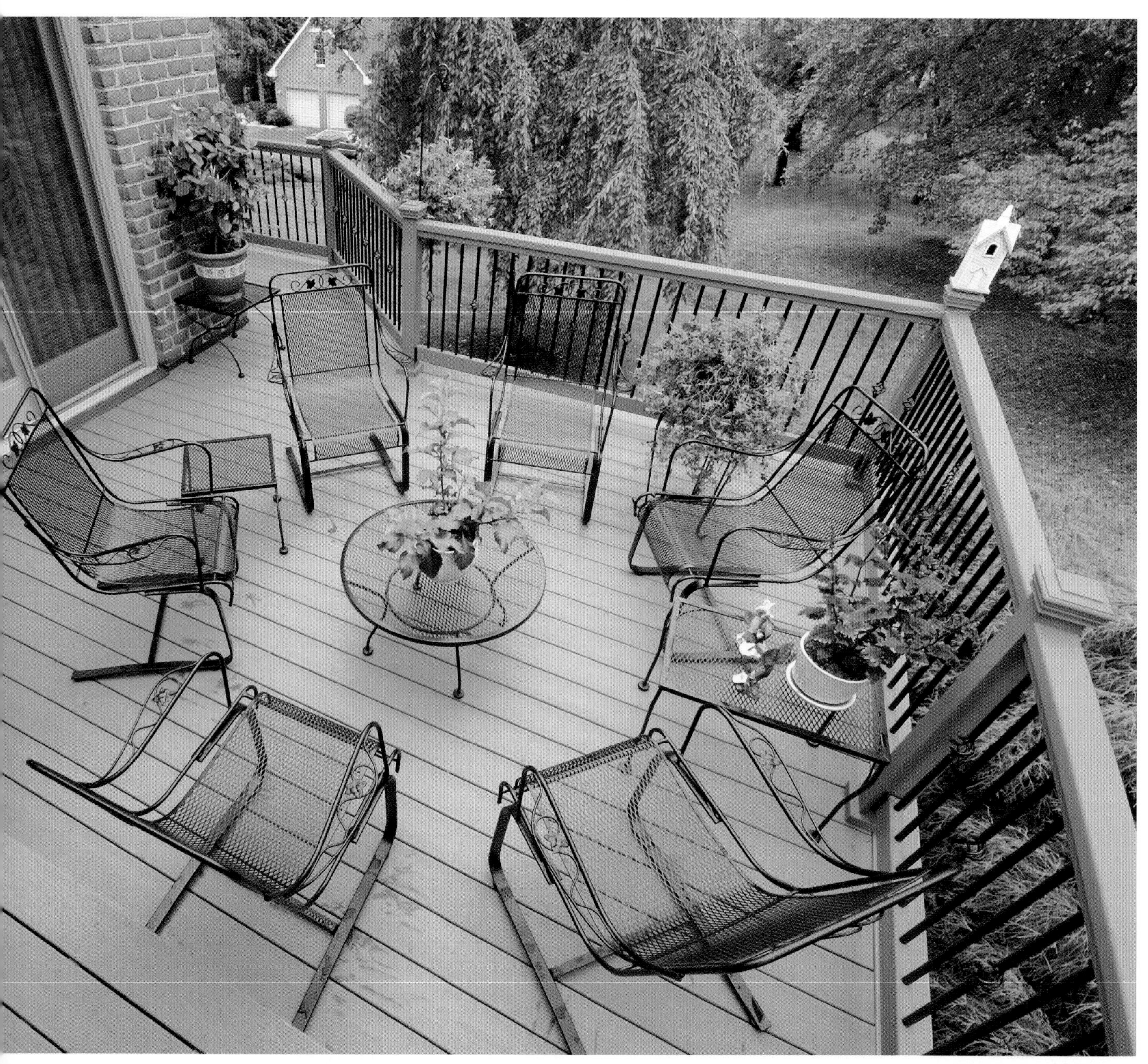

Think of a view as background. These homeowners chose to locate their deck on a corner overlooking their tree-studded backyard. Although they've created a conversation nook with a cluster of chairs and tables, the view is always there as a fabulous backdrop. When it comes to insightful deck design and placement, a great view will never go to waste.

Enjoying the View

Use views from ground level just like an elevated location. Any view seen from below can be as powerful as the same view from above. Physical beauty rises up on all sides of this multilevel deck, with intensely landscaped scenery filling the field of vision no matter where a visitor might look. The flowering hillsides compete for attention with the pool, but the winner is anyone enjoying the show from a chair on the deck.

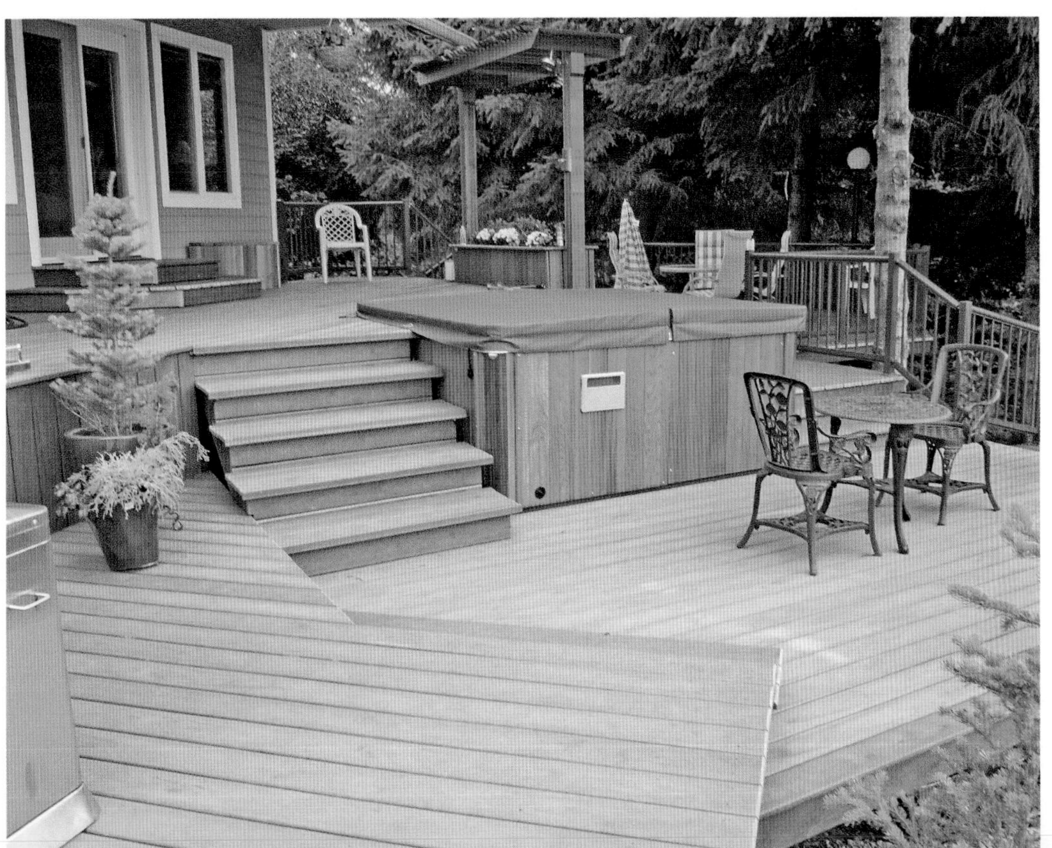

Get the most from a surrounding view with multiple levels. Although it would have been easier and less expensive for this homeowner to build a single-level deck, by choosing a multilevel design they ensured that each area of the deck has a different and interesting vantage point. There isn't a bad seat in the house—or outside of it.

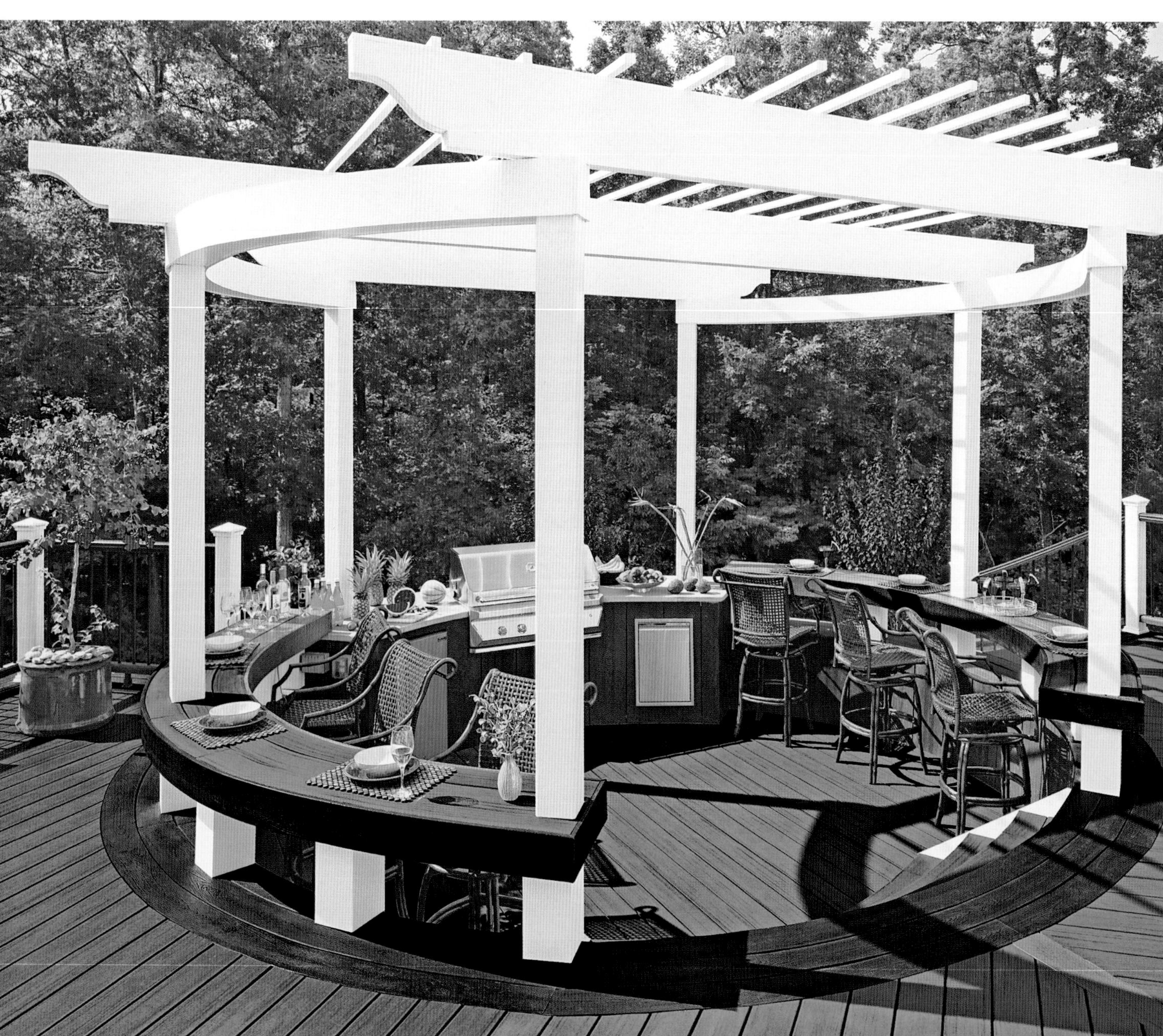

Outfit a complete outdoor kitchen and dining deck if you're a gourmet cook or devoted foodie. Although a fully functional outdoor kitchen requires much more planning than other types of decks—details such as hardwired electricity and possibly other utilities become essential—the return on investment can be huge. A well-equipped kitchen such as this one, with range and refrigerator, can make the deck even more enjoyable and usable. In temperate parts of the country, functional outdoor spaces like this will see use nearly year-round and could even challenge the primary kitchen for dominance.

Cover an outdoor kitchen to make preparing meals more comfortable and extend the season. An overhang such as this also defines the cooking area, setting it apart from the lower dining level. The deck builder has set aside abundant room for food preparation and to allow more than one person to work in the outdoor kitchen at a time.

Let the cook enjoy the deck as much as the guests do. The meals are a pleasure to prepare in this elegant space, but the kitchen and workspace has an unfettered view out into the well-landscaped yard. The kitchen itself is luxurious, outfitted with a cooktop, sink, prep area, and just about anything a cook might need. Comfort is assured as well, thanks to a two-tier pergola overhang that provides dappled shade.

Create visual interest by designing it with intersecting angles. The unique layout of this attention-grabbing deck makes clear separations between individual areas, including a spa tub alcove, a dining room, a conversation pit, and a cooking area. Clearly defining different areas of a multiuse deck is key to making it enjoyable and useful to everyone.

Gain separation between different areas by choosing a focal point. This is an especially effective strategy with single-level decks, such as the one shown here. The centerpiece makes for a natural positioning of the other areas and draws attention to the feature or purpose you intend to use the most.

Multipurpose Decks

Support multiple uses by creating cascading levels. The three levels of this deck are all clearly parts of a whole, but the central dining octagon is complemented by a general drinks and group social area at the bottom and an intimate conversation pit at the top. The deck makes the absolute most out of limited space by going vertical.

Go big if you have the budget. If you're willing to invest in a deck that you expect to use almost year-round, the sky is the limit to the number of uses it can accommodate. This multifunctional platform includes integrated—rather than clearly separated—areas. The hot tub shares space with the fire pit (a natural marriage), and seating areas are clustered around a bar and outdoor kitchen area, making the transition from dining to partying to socializing seamless.

DECK ACCESSIBILITY

Deck design, like all other design having to do with any structure in or attached to a house, is increasingly taking into account the specific needs of universal design and aging-in-place principles. Both of these movements focus on making the structure as accessible and safe for as many different individuals as possible. That includes designing features for people with disabilities (universal design) and the elderly or others who are experiencing mobility and strength difficulties (aging-in-place). In deck design, this most often translates to easier ways for an affected person to get on and off the deck. The two types of accessibility features are mechanical devices and ramps. For most homeowners, a simple ramp is the easiest and least expensive option. However, if the homeowner or resident in the home has a serious disability and is confined to a wheelchair, a motorized lift may be the only realistic option.

Don't sacrifice beauty and elegance when designing a deck ramp. Although any deck ramp needs to adhere to local codes regarding slope and placement, there are still many creative ways to integrate a ramp into a handsome deck. The deck shown here is a perfect example. The gorgeous hardwood structure dedicates the ramp as the only means of access to the deck proper (stairs lead to the door). The ramp has been built with a fascia and lattice skirting and deck surface that matches the deck itself. It's a natural look, and naturally beautiful.

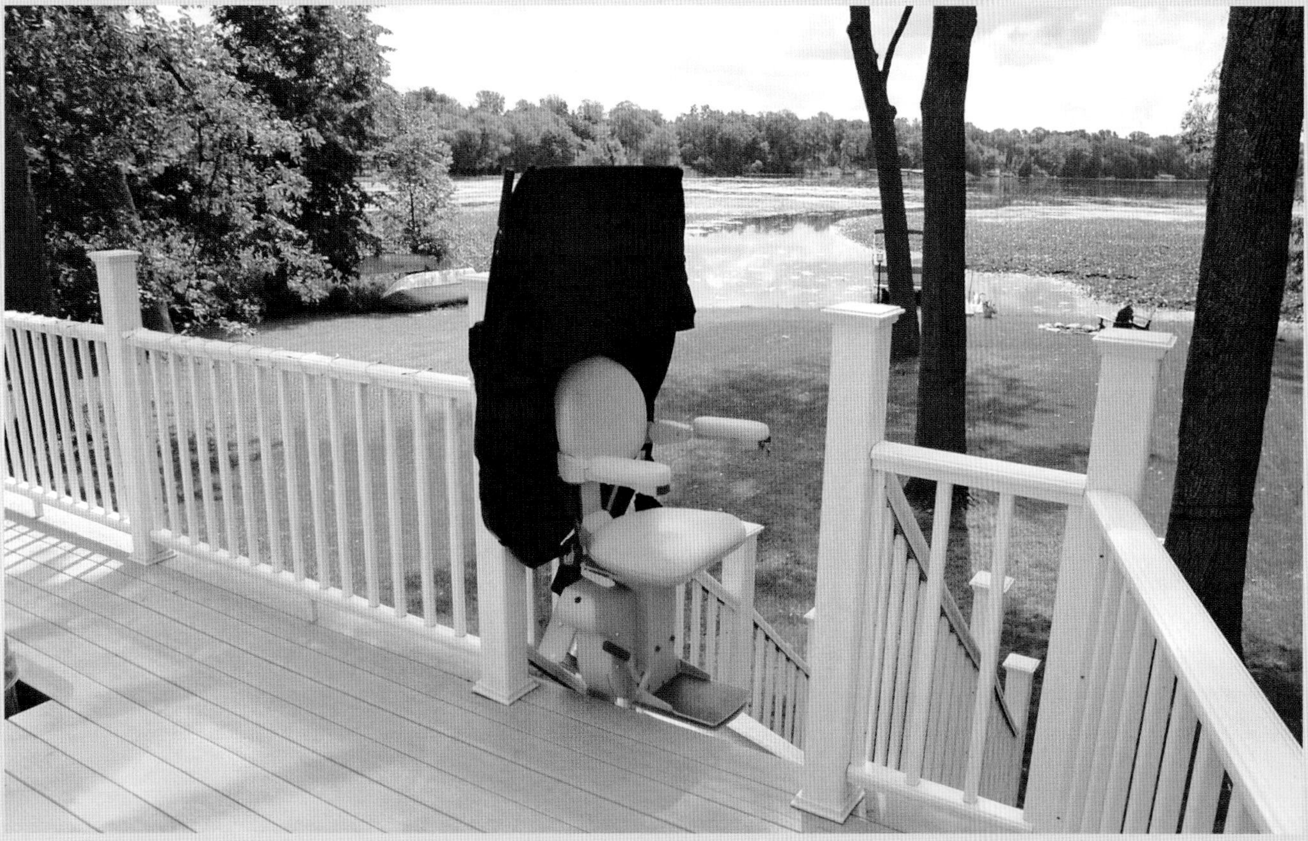

Improve deck stairs with an outdoor stairlift. A stairlift like this is a wonderful addition to a deck used regularly by the elderly or anyone with a lower-body condition that makes mobility difficult. This chair, like most outdoor stairlifts, folds up and out of the way when not in use, allowing easy passage on the stairs. The chair also comes with a cover to keep it in good shape over colder months or when the weather is inclement.

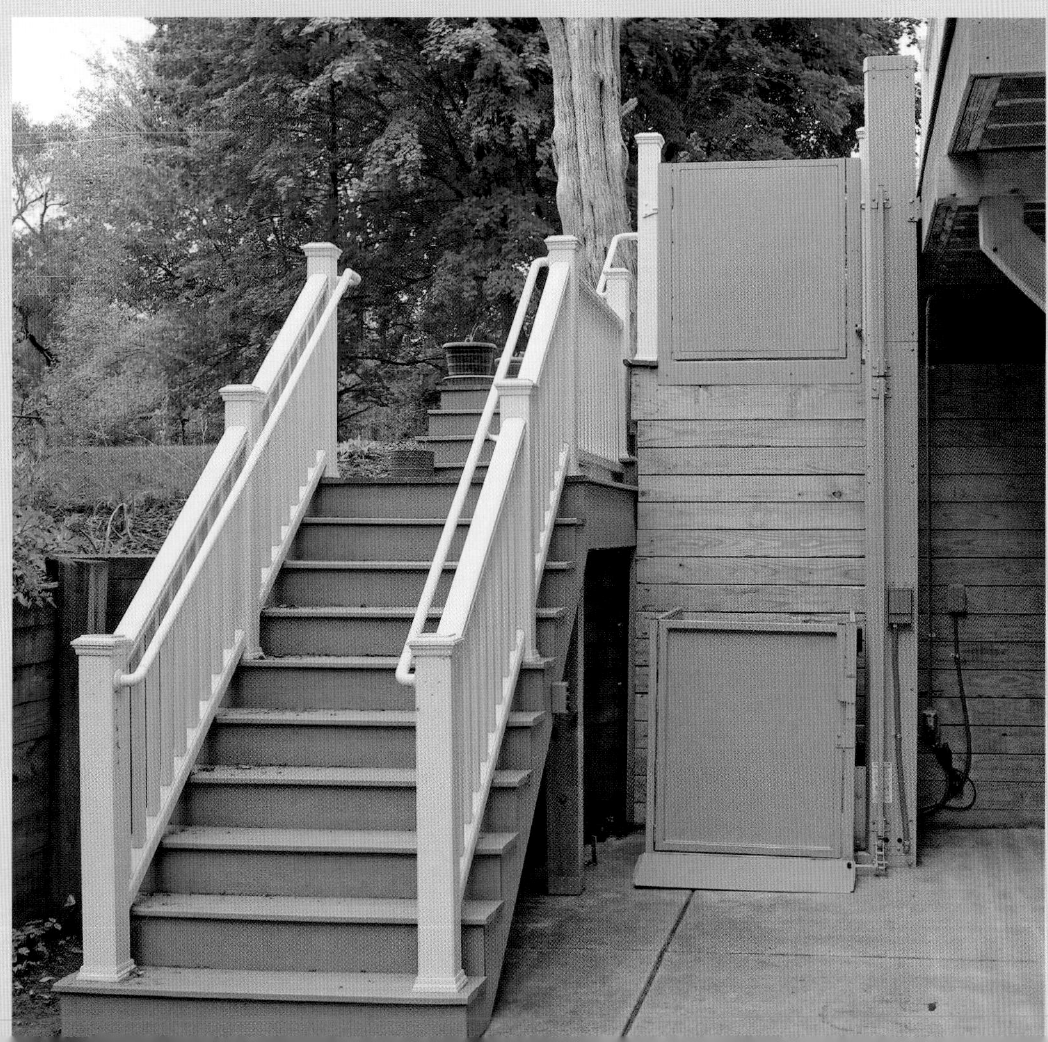

Lift those that need help directly up to the surface of tall, elevated decks. Outdoor elevators like this are proven means of access on decks that are too high, or where the person is too weak, for a ramp to make sense. Like a stairlift, the elevator needs power and professional installation, but today's models are remarkably durable and reliable.

DECK FEATURES

Just like clothes make the man, design details make the deck. Although there's no crime in building a simple, plain platform to take advantage of a backyard view, or as a no-frills summer hangout to share a few drinks with friends, it's the very rare deck that isn't improved with one or more built-in features.

Some of these are required. Handrails, for instance, are mandated by local codes for decks a certain height above the ground. Stairs are simply practical necessities for elevated or multilevel decks. As practical as these features may be, however, they can also be built with incredible style.

Other deck additions serve specific needs. Light fixtures, a privacy fence, or a pergola that breaks up the direct sun exposure over a spa tub will make your deck much more comfortable. Some features bridge that line between function and looks. Benches are a prime example. Although they supply a practical place to sit down, they are not, strictly speaking, necessary.

Other features are more—or completely—aesthetic in nature. A planter or a fire pit makes a deck more enchanting and makes the time you spend there more pleasant. Inlaid designs gracing the surface of a deck are likewise simple decorations. But when you're dealing with what can be such a plain feature in the yard, these types of treatments can have tremendous impact.

That's why no matter what built-in feature you're considering for your deck design, always keep appearances in mind. No feature on a deck should look like an afterthought. As much as a wonderful latticework fence can add to a deck, a poorly designed, tacked-on bench or overhang will surely detract from it.

Make steep staircases seem less daunting. The designer of this composite deck interrupted the staircase with a landing halfway down the run to give a more pleasing appearance to the stairs, and make them easier to climb as well. Wraparound stairs such as these also make the deck more accessible and modern-looking.

Railings

Make deck railings pop by using contrast. The black of these metal balusters, post caps, and rail hangers all stand out against the tan of the composite decking and wood of the railings themselves. The railing gets a splash of added flair with scroll-worked baluster accents. Because it is so apparent, this type of detail carries a lot of weight in how the deck will be perceived.

Exploit the malleability of iron for showcase balusters. These supporting players have been bent to a distinctive shape, one that draws the eye along the railing. Notice that the designer used balusters of the same shape; varying the shapes would have created visual chaos. The builder also paid attention to the fine details, such as attaching the balusters with screws that have blackened heads—successfully avoiding eyesores that might mar the look.

Bring a railing to life with vivid pairings. The clean white and sharp, glossy black of this railing pop out against the neutral tan of the deck. The deck, rails, and posts are all composite materials, which translates to a lower cost of fabrication than if the railings were constructed of hardwood. It also means the railings will look sharp for years to come with minimal maintenance.

Sprinkle in a unique element with a specialized baluster. Iron, metal, and aluminum balusters come in a variety of wrought designs, such as the twisting spiral shown here. Choose the number of decorative balusters you want to include in each section of railing and order them from the manufacturer for your own signature look. Want to go even more custom? Have metal balusters bent to your specifications by a metal shop.

Leverage natural beauty with classic, wrought-iron balusters. The unadorned lines of this staircase serve as a foil for the wavy contours of the iron balusters. The wood's dull brown surface is more attractive when played against the metal's gloss black finish. Not only is the look much sharper than all-wood pieces would have been, the rail-attached balusters are simple to install.

Ensure safety as much as aesthetics on pool decks. The railing here keeps children on the deck, while looking great with post-cap lights in the color of the balusters, and decorative baluster accents. But the most important feature of this particular railing is the safety gate that has been crafted to blend in with the railings themselves. It's not only a good idea, it's code in many areas.

Mount railings on the deck fascia. As shown here, this mounting style is modern and maximizes the floor space of the deck. But be sure to check and follow local codes—the posts must be mounted in a secure fashion to prevent accidents.

Pay a bit more for craftsmanship. The post in this stained hardwood rail has been run up through the top rail fillet—rather than the more conventional practice of simply attaching the fillets to the side of the post. The post has been topped with a hand-turned finial. The detail is amazing, and the precision of the construction is sure to draw rave reviews.

Railings

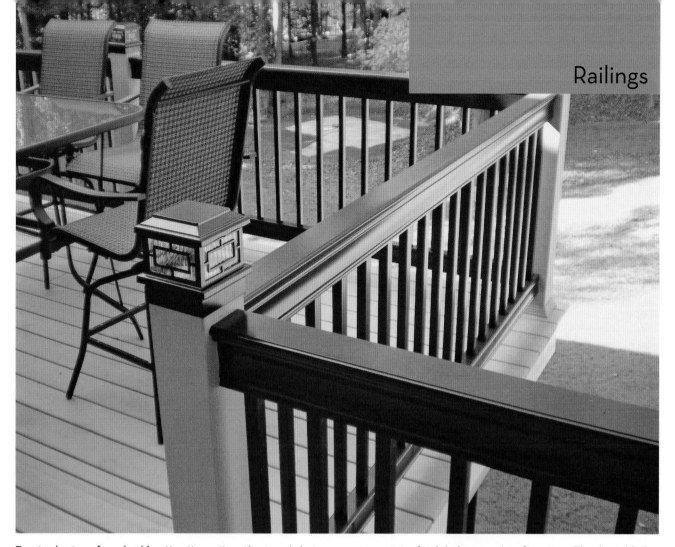

Turn to aluminum for a durable, attractive option. Aluminum balusters come in a variety of stylish shapes and configurations. The classic black-and-tan finishing on this railing is powder coated to hold up against years of weather and deck use. Aluminum railings also come with the same accessories featured on composite and wood railings. This particular construction incorporates stunning post-cap lights that add panache as well as illumination.

Combine different materials for a simply stunning rail. This handcrafted wood railing features old-world touches that play against the look of high-tech stainless-steel tube balusters. It's a highly unusual look, but one that works well. Railings are a great place to try out innovative combinations such as this, because they are so easily changed if the combinations don't work.

Dress up posts with fancy lighting fixtures. Today's manufacturers offer a variety of railing lighting fixtures, providing you with exceptional design flexibility. Composite posts, such as the one shown here, are usually constructed hollow or with a channel that allows for hardwired fixtures. This post features a decorative "sleeve" light on the top, and a mounted hood fixture for lighting up the deck's surface.

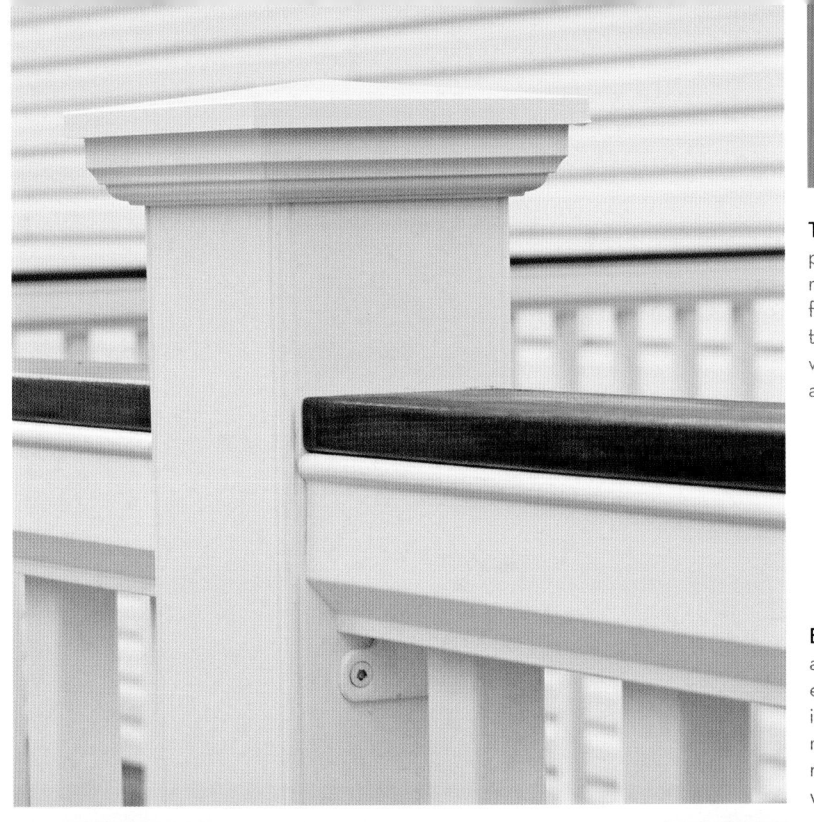

Railings

Tap the amazing possibilities of composite railings. The potential design variations among composite railings matches that in decking options. This composite post features a highly detailed post cap, with rail fasteners that blend in wonderfully and a composite top-rail fillet with wood grain and color. The look is tasteful, refined, and easy to create.

Blend the railing into the deck with color. This unusual, almost gold railing is the perfect complement to the especially light color and wood graining of the deck itself. Both are composites supplied by the same manufacturer. Composite railings can be colored in many different hues, even though black, browns, and white are the most popular.

Make a bold statement with your post. Stone posts, such as the one shown here, can add a distinguished feel to any railing. As this one shows, stone also blends well with the wood components of a railing. This is actually a prefab stone post, with a sleek, wired-in metal light fixture that adds a tiny accent to the look of the deck.

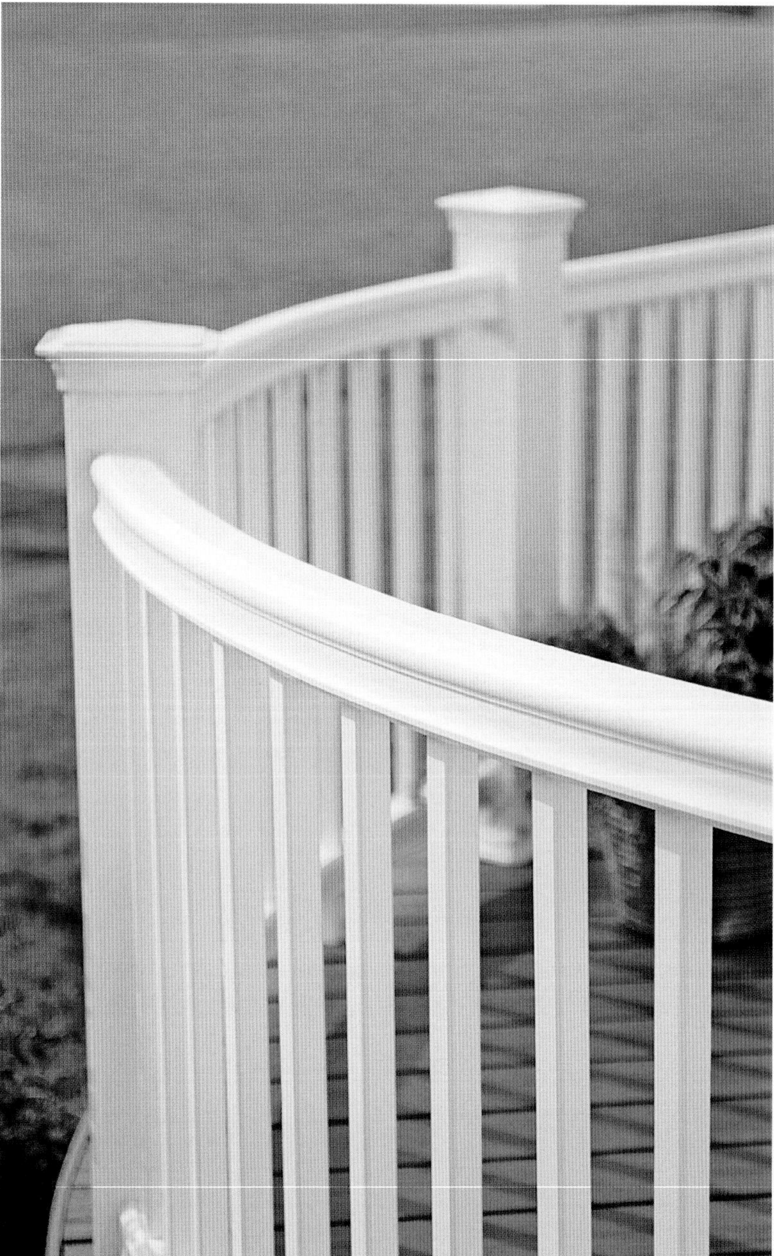

A curved railing is the best partner for a round deck edge. This particular curve is made easier to construct with the use of composite materials. Composite manufacturers can actually extrude the railing in the shape of the curve, making for a fairly simple installation. Composite materials present many dynamic railing design opportunities.

Pay attention to the fine points. Small details can make the look of a deck, and few details are so front-and-center as railing accents. This white composite post was constructed with molding that mimics a millworked footing. Notice that the connection between bottom rail and post is finished with the same treatment, all of which gives the post and railing an incredibly polished appearance.

Choose a Craftsman-style railing. As this post clearly shows, a handmade railing can include details no prefabricated type can match. The builder of this deck included details such as pegged construction, thick rope handrail, and millworked post top. A custom steel pyramid cap is the icing on a spectacular railing design.

Establish crisply modern looks. Using exposed "button" fasteners for the cable railing ends is an easy way to add small splashes of style. As shown on the end post for this beige composite railing, fasteners in a different color stand out rather than blending with the post—the traditional way of treating hardware.

Be bold in your choice of colors. Powder-coated aluminum railings such as this open up a whole world of color possibilities when it comes to your deck design. This fun, vivid, plum-colored railing is just one of many shades available in aluminum railings. This version is well suited as a partner to an unconventional sheet vinyl membrane deck surface. The whole look is upbeat and different.

Railings

Secure an utterly sleek, cutting-edge look. These panels are tempered safety glass that reduces the risk of injury in the event of an accident. They are also incredibly beautiful, drawing attention to themselves only as the deck is perceived as a whole; at other times, they are merely windows to the backyard view and nearly invisible barriers helping define the deck's shape.

Block out part of a view with a machined-glass railing panel. The sitting area on this deck looks out over the water, but unattractive homes below clutter the view. The solution is to block the homes and leave the water, with glass panels that featured a texture surface. The panels allow for light but block the undesirable part of the view.

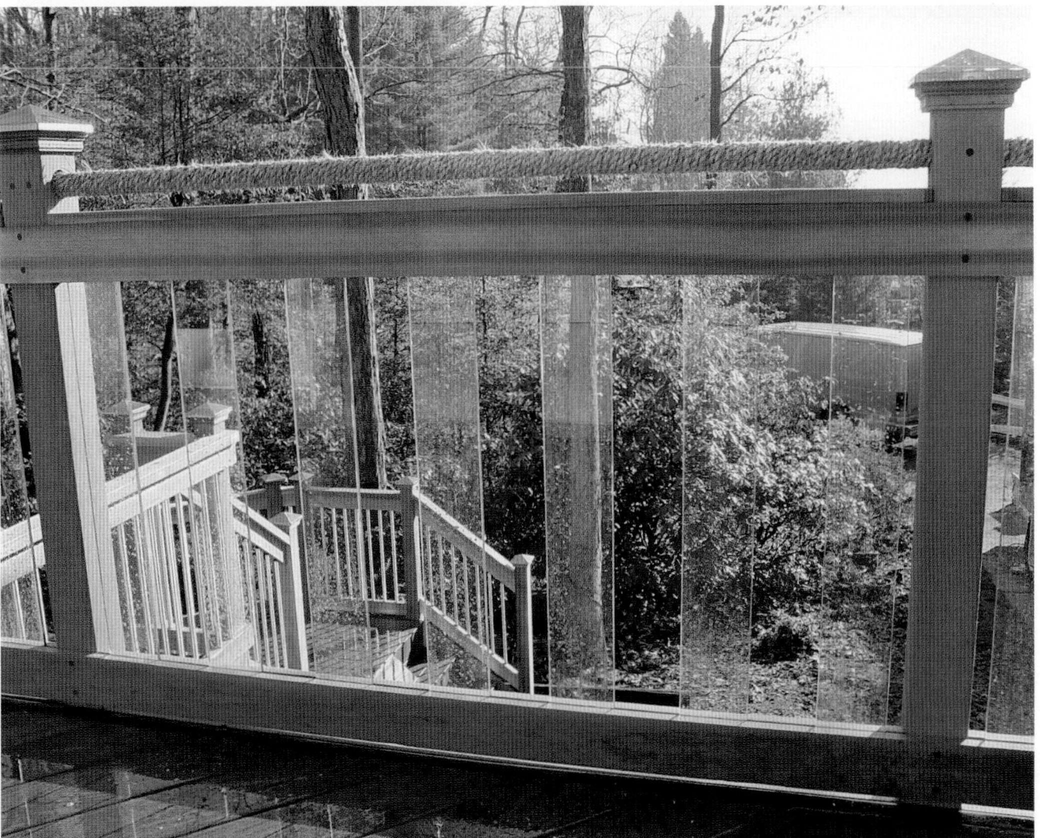

Juxtapose materials to create intense interest. This is another way to use glass panels in a deck railing—as balusters. Although full panels are more commonly used, the builder of this deck used strips of glass in this handcrafted, custom wood railing. Be careful to maintain balance in a design like this. Here, the wood and its details dominate, with the glass serving as a supporting player.

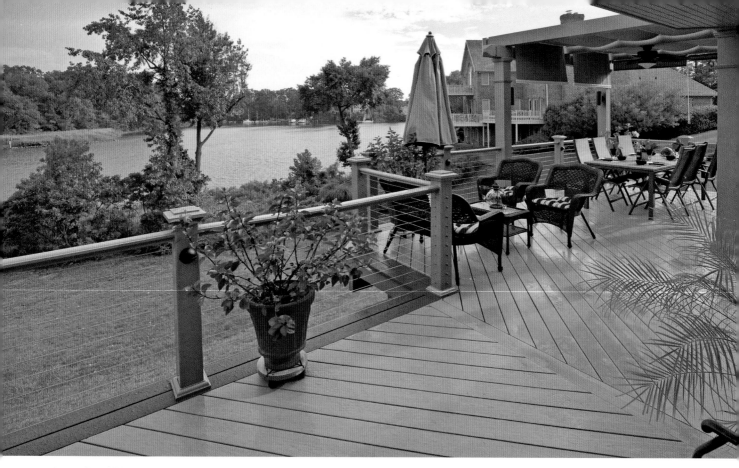

Pair railing cables with relatively plain posts. The twisted steel cables in this railing catch light in different ways over the course of the day, offering a changeable graphic element. Ball-type fasteners used at the end of cable runs, mounted on the opposite side of the post to secure the cables, put the look over the top. The design element adds immeasurably to what is a subtly sophisticated overall aesthetic.

Marry cabled railing to dark-stained hardwood posts. Stainless-steel cable is a natural partner to dark wood, as is clear here, and the combination creates a sleek, modern look. The pairing is incredibly powerful when the post and top rails are kept basic, with flat angular forms like the ones used in this structure. The house may not be a modern style like the railings, but the clean, spare lines of cabled railings go well with just about any type of architecture.

Rescue any deck from a boring look with cabled railings. This deck and stairs were designed to blend into the wooded hillside, and the construction is rather plain. But the use of cables in the railings adds a spark to the look of the deck. As a bonus, the cables used in different areas catch sun at different times, visually reading as lighter or darker at any given moment.

Up the excitement factor by mixing and matching elements. The technique has to be done carefully to work, but the result can be impressive. This cabling is so minimal that is doesn't clash with the other elements, as standard balusters might have. Use different colors in posts and rails for a dynamic look. This one is accented by black rail hangers and post-mounted lights.

Don't make design statements where they're not necessary. This is no more true than when you're working with a material that is already attention-grabbing in its own right. This attractive wood railing matches the deck, creating a pleasant visual continuity. The actual design of the railing is fairly simple and straightforward. That means it not only complements the overall look of the structure, it also facilitates ease of construction.

Rock a monochromatic railing for a calm, understated look. Here, a white railing seems to pop out of the neutral-toned deck, with a traditional, dignified form that adds some measure of class and style to the deck. But mostly, the standardized form is easy on the eyes, allowing the compelling view from the deck to dominate the scene.

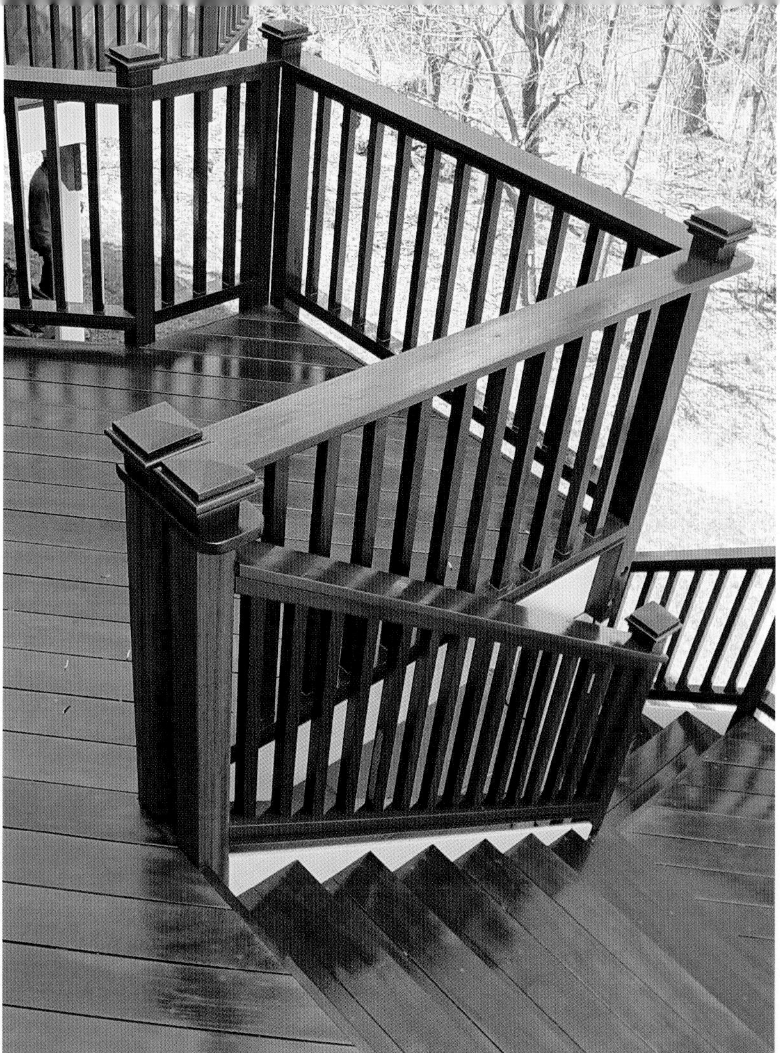

Railings

Extend the look of a dramatic deck. The exceptional hardwood deck shown here was stained dark and finished with a high-gloss coating. The same finish was used on the railings. The grain patterns and deep color work with fine details such as millworked post caps to create a lasting impression of unrivaled sophistication.

Spruce up ordinary woods with extraordinary design. Pressure-treated pine railings can be a bit utilitarian, but not when you paint the deck and top fillet a plum color as the builder of this structure did. He also incorporated a traditional "Chippendale" pattern inside the railing. Regardless of the material you're using for the railing construction, a pattern such as this adds an incredible amount of visual interest.

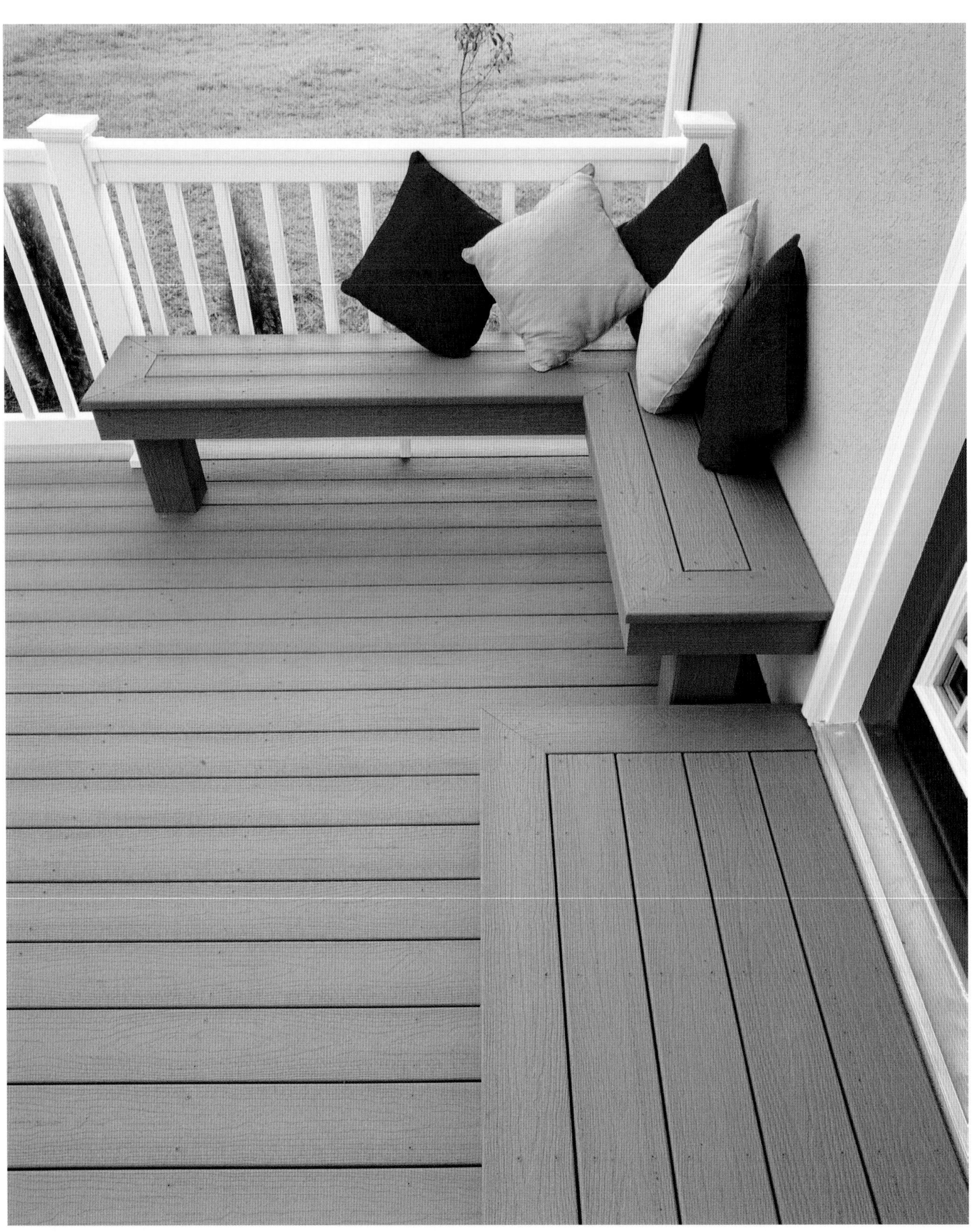

Go simple with built-in seating. This gray composite deck includes a blocky L bench in one corner. The positioning is not accidental; by running one leg of the L along the house wall, the bench has a natural back surface against which people can lean, making the seating more comfortable and usable.

Seating

Use benches and railings to define the border of unusual deck shapes, or those nestled in dense landscape. This is especially true where the deck will almost fade into naturalistic surroundings. The benches used here, and repeated at opposite corners, are slotted to allow the moisture inherent in the location to pass through without causing mold or rot problems.

Make the most of deck seating by adding functionality. A perfect example of hybrid function in a built-in feature, this simple bench has an ice cooler incorporated. The high-quality composite used for the deck and bench is resistant to rot, decay, water, and insect infiltration, making it an ideal material for the cooler.

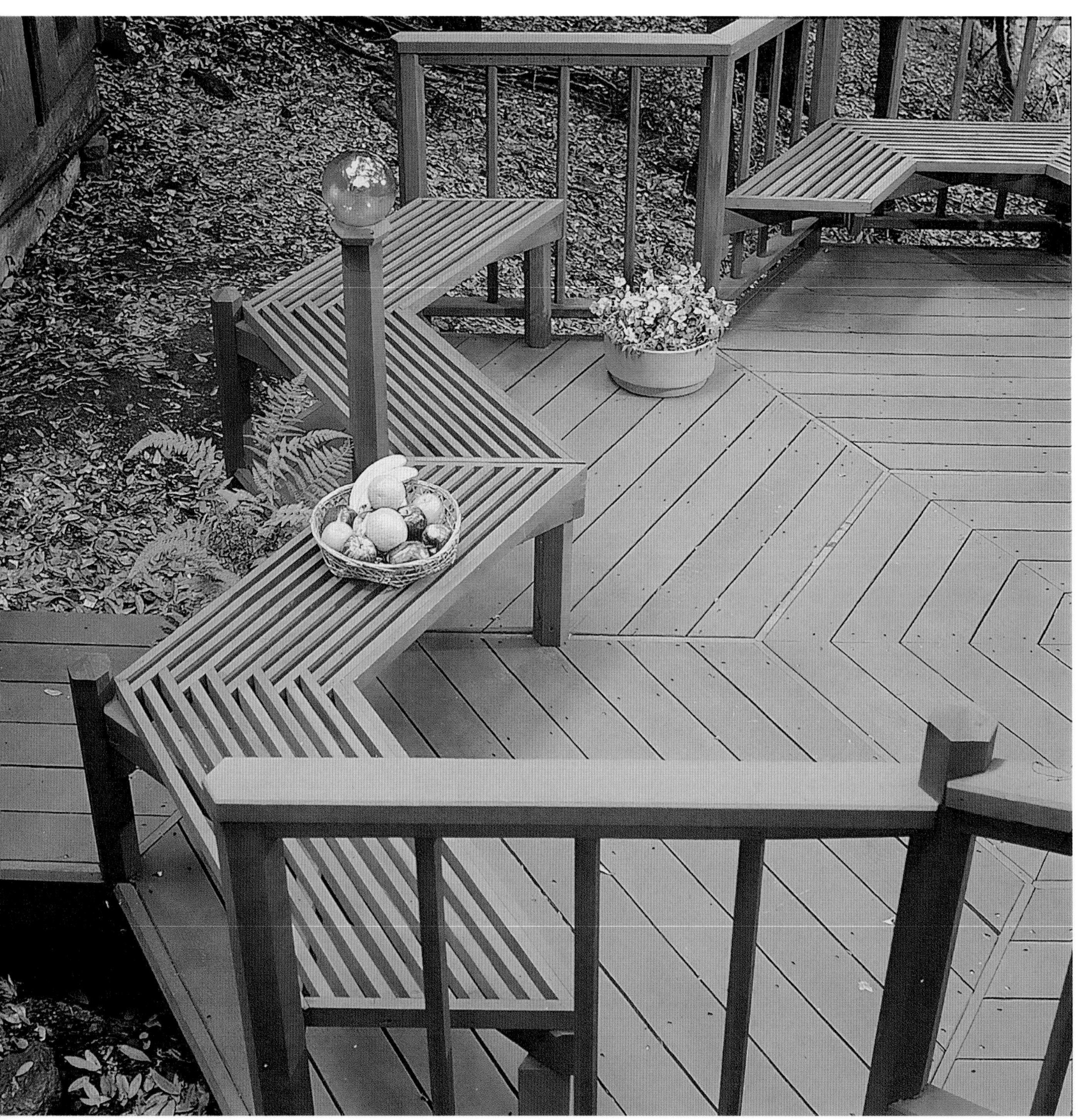

Design seating for the wow factor. The zigzag pattern of these benches makes for a very interesting look, as well as being far easier to install than curved or enclosed benches. The slats allow moisture to fall through the seats, and what remains causes little damage because the benches are made—like the deck below them—of clear heart redwood that is nearly impervious to rot and insect infestation.

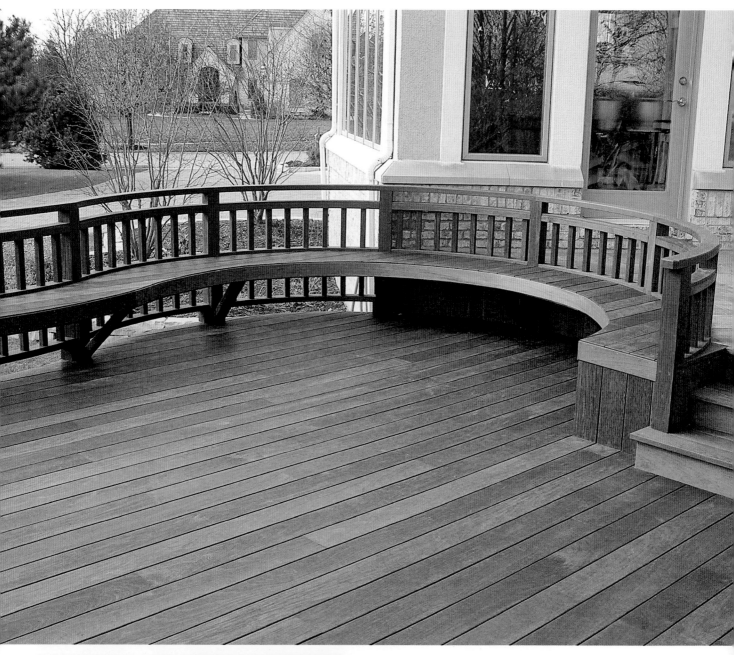

Add curved benches for a graceful element. This bench is made of the alluring hardwood ipe, and the open-design handrail that serves as a backing for the bench maintains visual flow and establishes a very sophisticated style that is right in keeping with the refined appearance of ipe's beautiful color and grain. Details like this evidence the hand of a fine craftsman and separate basic decks from really special and singular outdoor areas.

Use seating as accent. This deck was built around an old tree, with edge benches that give a finished appearance to the deck. But small built-in benches on either side of the tree also effectively frame the element and guide attention to what is really a living deck ornament. Other, moveable seating can be arranged as needed, but these benches remain nice places to relax in the shade.

Inject a spectacular design feature with a compass rose. An inlay such as this is as close to original art as deck building gets. The design was crafted of the same composite material as the deck itself, but required a skilled professional with the abilities necessary to make the fine cuts.

Complement a spectacular vista. The view of the mountains isn't the only gaze-grabbing feature of this composite deck. The lookout extension designed into the structure features an inlaid compass rose. This is one of the most common designs for deck inlays, both because it's a traditional design with storied nautical roots, and it's a simpler shape to actually inlay into the deck than one with many curves or intricate figures.

Inlays

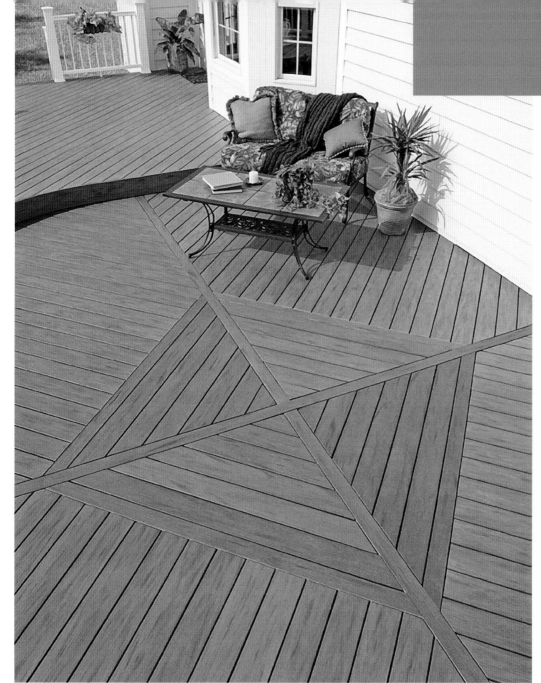

Enjoy the power of an inlay with a simple geometric design. Deck inlays don't need to be complex to have an impact. Even a fairly basic design adds variety and draws the eye to the deck's surface. This diamond was executed in a solid color that contrasted the overall decking, but the pattern is really quite basic, simply involving boards run in different directions and cut on the same angle at both ends.

Use composites for your inlay to open up the possibilities. The close-up here shows how the inlay is set into the deck; special blocking is needed to support the inlay and hidden fasteners supplied by the manufacturer have been used. What you can't see is that these boards are a different color on each face. This makes executing the design much simpler.

A winding walkway and broad stairs create a welcoming entry to any deck. This stately house would not be the same without the wide entryway adorned with a white deck rail. Although not everyone is a fan of vinyl deck rails, this example demonstrates that with some good design sense any material can contribute to the visual impact of a deck.

Configure stairs to suit your purposes. Here, a stately staircase of contrasting stained hardwood and white fascia boards follows an L run. The staircase wraps around a bland storage unit positioned under the deck. The positioning effectively hides the storage unit and shows off the craftsmanship apparent in such details as enclosed risers and handcrafted post caps.

Make a stair rail a style accent. Handrails required by local codes don't have to be an afterthought. This ipe handrail has been stained and finished with a gloss coating that shouts chic. The handrail pops even more, framed as it is against balusters in contrasting bright white. Just one more case where safety and looks go hand in hand.

Grace a traditional deck with traditional stairs. These steps could have been constructed with open risers (code would have allowed it), but the look would have jarringly contrasted the finished appeal of the rest of the deck. Instead, risers that match the fascia boards, and steps in the same material as the decking, create a very polished look.

Capture the eye with curves. This type of construction takes a bit more time and expertise, but it pays big rewards in the form of a graceful appearance far beyond what you would expect on such a modest deck. In fact, the scalloped edge is what brings this deck to life, and the stairs are a big part of that flair.

Strive to integrate stairs with the design. The technique used here is a common one on upscale contemporary decks. The steps are built to entirely surround the perimeter of the deck, looking almost like layers or edging. A border of decorative stone adds to the effect and provides a pretty transition between the deck steps and the grass.

Make your stairs go in two different directions. A "bridge" staircase such as this is a wonderful way to terminate a long flight of stairs so that traffic is directed two ways. In this case, the stairs allow access from the lawn or a lower patio, increasing accessibility with a high-style construction.

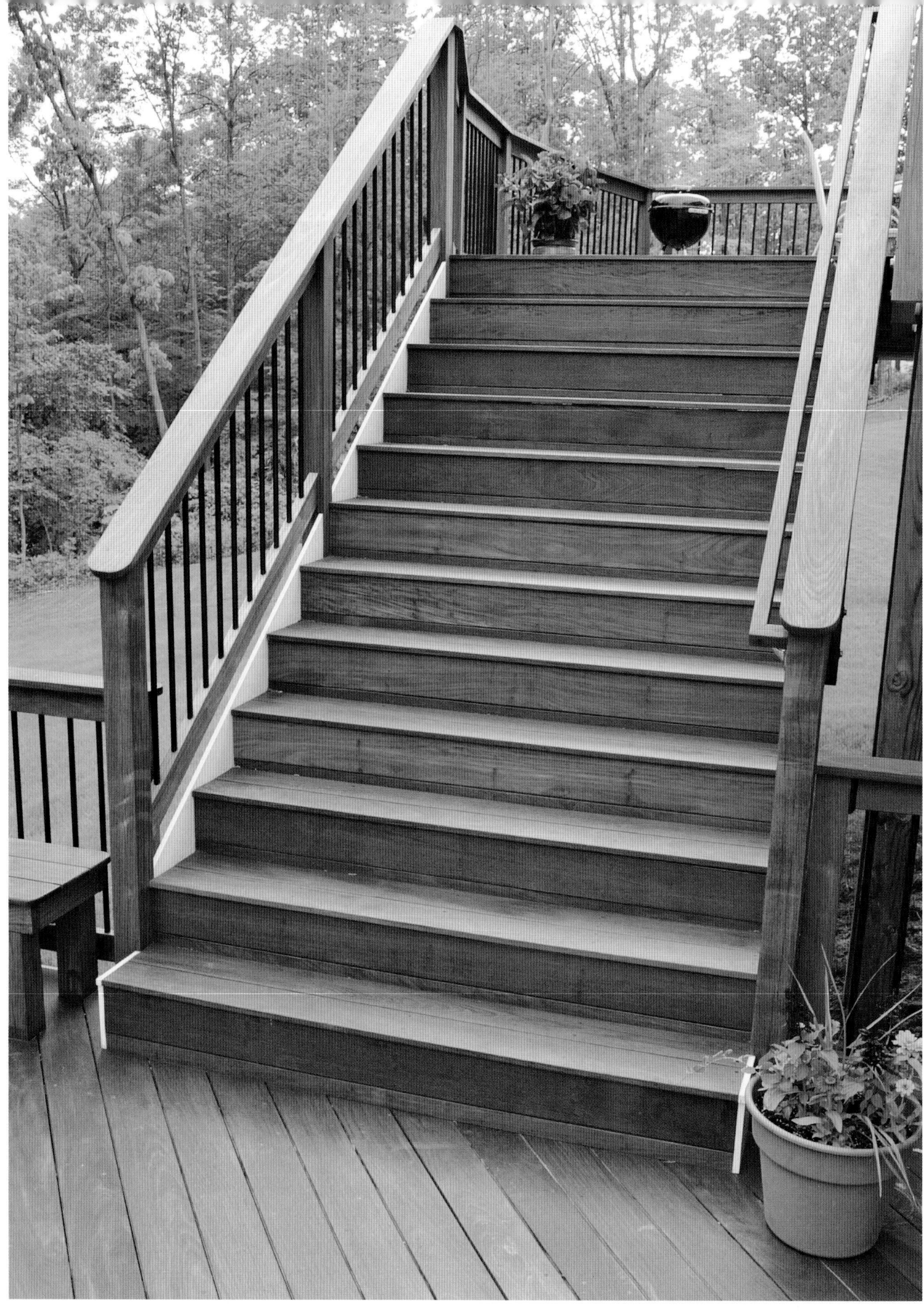

Use small touches to provide the flair. This basic staircase allows the beauty of the hardwood to dominate. The handrails are unadorned with flat fillets terminating in rounded edges that are pleasant to the touch. A white sideboard encloses the steps, but it's a clean look. A separate handrail adds safety. The staircase is handsome without calling attention to itself.

Stairs

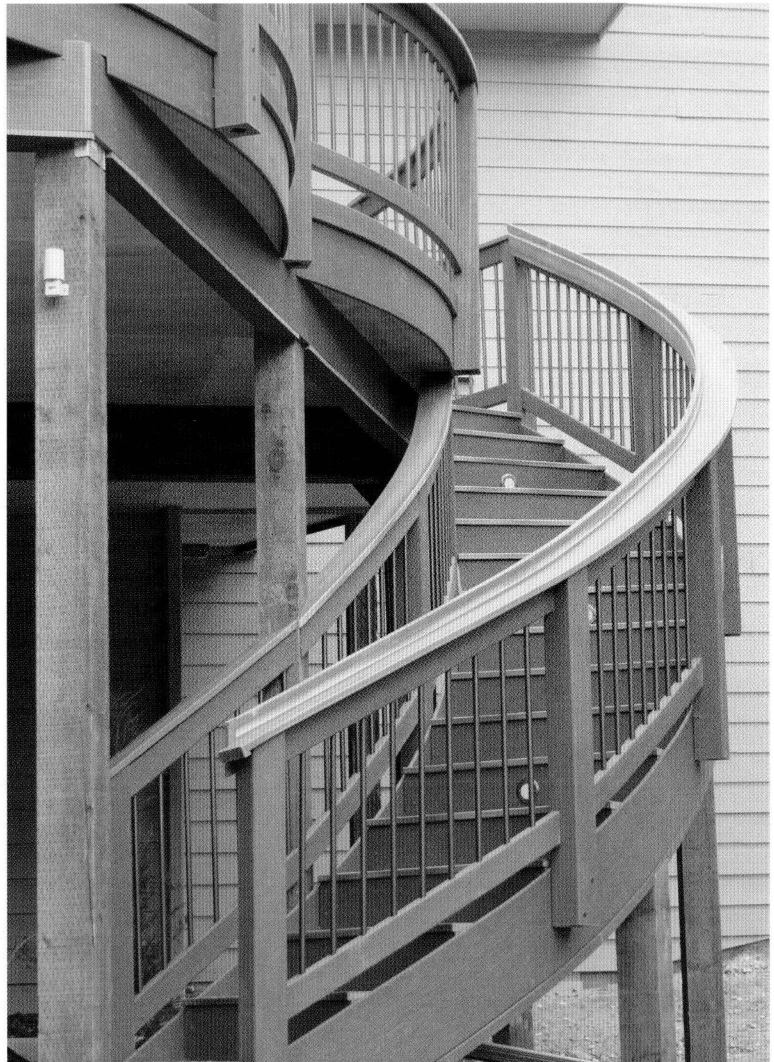

Install a spiral staircase where vertical space is tight and you want to incorporate a distinctive design element. These types of staircases can be fascinating focal points. The stairs should be carefully designed for optimum spacing (or you can buy a prefab type made to your specifications). Here, the staircase mimics the curves of the deck itself and is made of the same material, establishing a pleasing visual continuity.

Break up a long run of stairs. When the terrain calls for a long descent, it's wise to interrupt the stairs visually and physically with a sizable platform. A surface like the octagon shown here can actually become a functional level of the deck, but a smaller surface will be just as effective. The idea in either case is to break up the visual monotony of a long staircase and make it easier and safer to climb or descend.

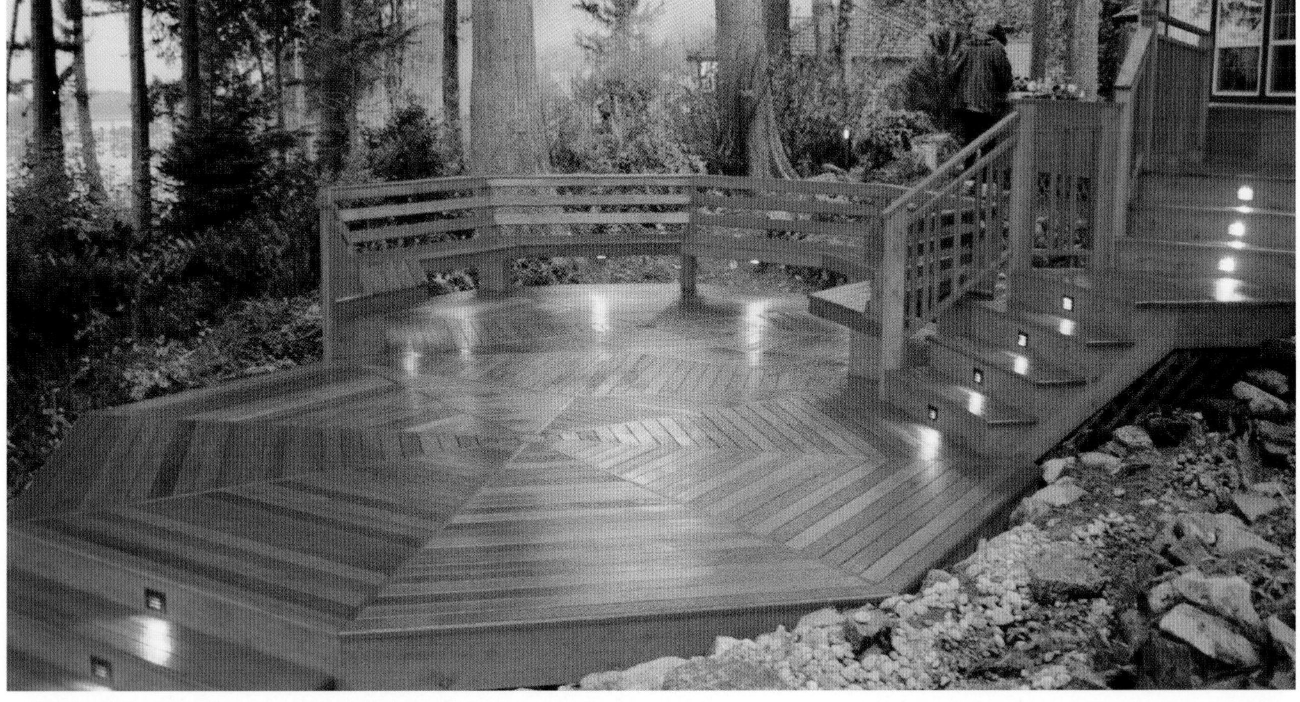

Add planters to counter a bland look. Planters are a natural accompaniment to built-in deck benches. The most common treatment is to run the bench into a planter as the builder did here. The corner planter is an independent feature. But butting the bench end right up against the planter creates the pleasing visual impression that the two are a single feature.

Say "welcome" with a pair of planters. These simple planters—essentially boxes with holes cut in the top to accommodate terra cotta pots—did not break the bank for the homeowner and provided a lot of bang for the buck. Seasonal flowers in bloom become an invitation to walk up the stairs and enjoy the deck. It's a nice symmetry that any deck can include.

Break up spans of a low deck with planters. Handrails are not required by most codes for a small, low deck such as this. But left bare, the deck would seem incomplete. Using built-in features around the border of the deck encloses it and makes it feel self-contained and cozy.

Built in at regular intervals around the perimeter, planters become a pleasing design element. They also allow for lush flora that softens the normally hard edges of a deck. The composite materials used in both the deck and planters here make fabrication easy and helped the homeowner achieve a crisp look in the planters and supported benches between them.

Choose plants wisely. In the end, any planter box is meant to be planted. The large and deep planter on this deck provides plenty of space for the soil needed to support a gorgeous profusion of trailing annuals and perennials. The planter sides were crafted to match the angle and material used in the skirting and house siding, making it seem to spring up out of the deck.

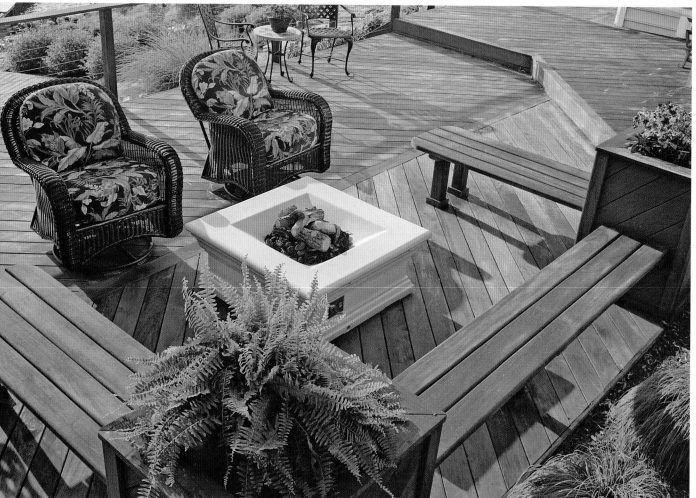

Use corner planters as anchors. The planters here are built of the same hardwood as the deck and benches, but stand tall and help define this social corner grouped around a fire pit. The builder has run the boards that make up the planters' sides at a diagonal to make them stand out a bit.

Planters

Look for a touch of design flair. This bench is run into the planter, providing anyone that sits on it with the company of lovely flowers. But the designer has added a bit of whimsy by terminating the opposite end of the bench in a point. Small touches like this can make the look of a deck.

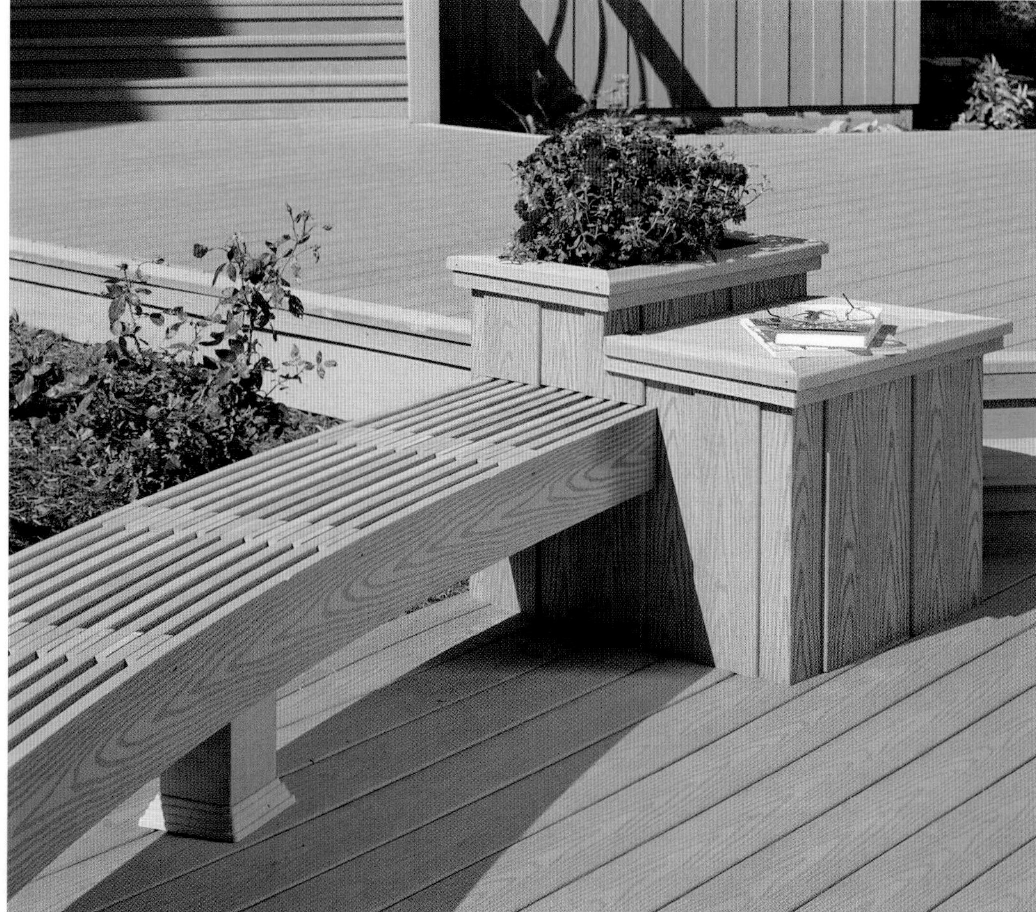

Integrate planters with other structures. The designer of this deck didn't settle for a lovely flowering addition to a slotted bench; he extended the planter to create a built-in side table. The result is a useful and unique feature that perfectly supplements the graceful construction of the bench.

Enhance any dining deck with a stunning, sturdy pergola. This pergola was built by an experienced craftsman, and the details show the professional touch. Faux footings were created at the base of the supporting posts, and a series of cut-ins decorate the crossbeam ends. Diners benefit from the sun-blocking shade sails—in matching color—draped across the joists.

Choose composite materials to complement your decking. As shown in the details apparent here, composite manufacturers can supply elegant pergola framing members that are finely crafted, durable, and super attractive. The white color is a great choice as well, to avoid fading.

Pergolas & Overhangs

Distinguish a pergola and make it a standout feature. Squared, painted columns hold rafters finished natural with ends cut in a wave design. The rafters are crossed on top with decorative members that add another layer to the design. A mix of shapes and contrasting finishes are design techniques used to create lively and interesting pergolas.

Showcase a little artistic elegance in your pergola. This deck was already special, with a hardwood surface and a pergola roof complemented by posts and balusters painted a very sophisticated gray. The builder added a showstopping centerpiece in the form of a pagoda-style topper mounted on the pergola's joists. The effect is at once refined and powerful.

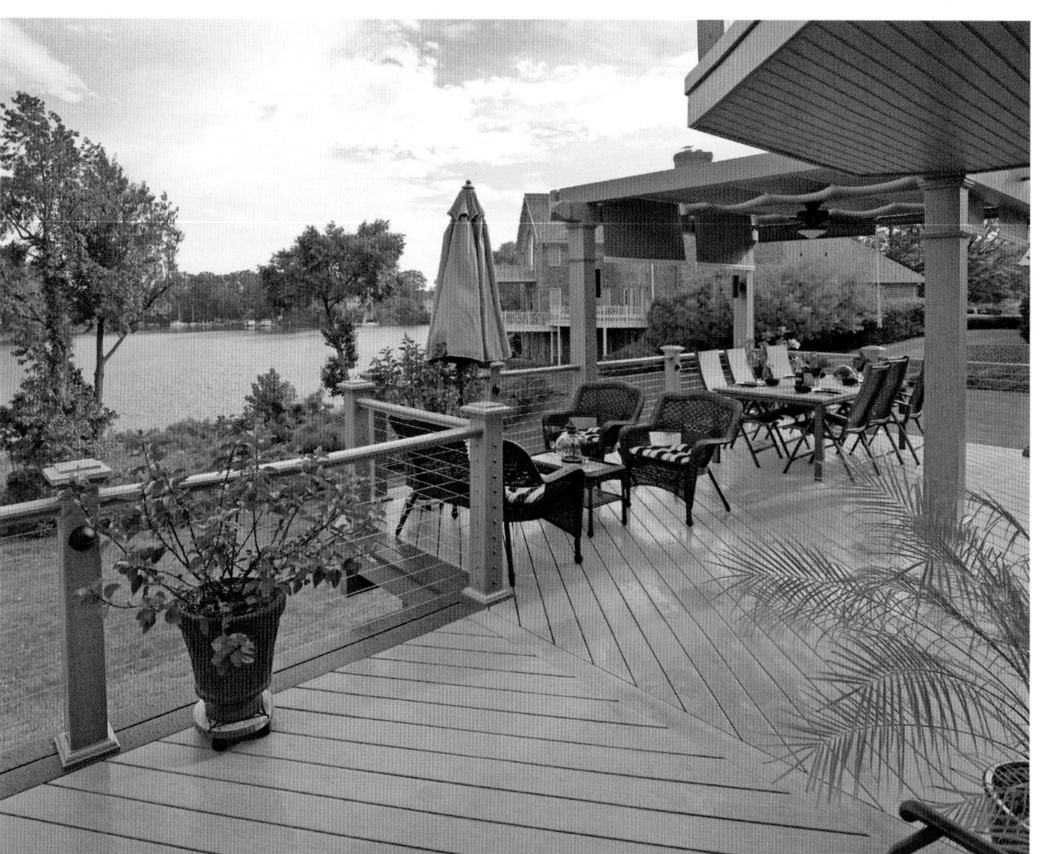

Design a pergola for both function and form. The solid, blocky construction of this pergola gives the whole deck a feeling of substance and weight even though it is elevated. Simple canvas shade sails in a matching color provide protection from the strong sun of the southeasterly exposure.

Pergolas & Overhangs

Use the pergola in more than one season. The gaps between pergola joists can create fascinating shadows, but if you want a three-season deck space, those gaps can be a problem. The owner of this deck solved that problem with clear fiberglass panels attached to the crosspieces that lay perpendicular to the pergola's joists. The space enjoys a wealth of light when it's sunny, and protection from the elements when it's not.

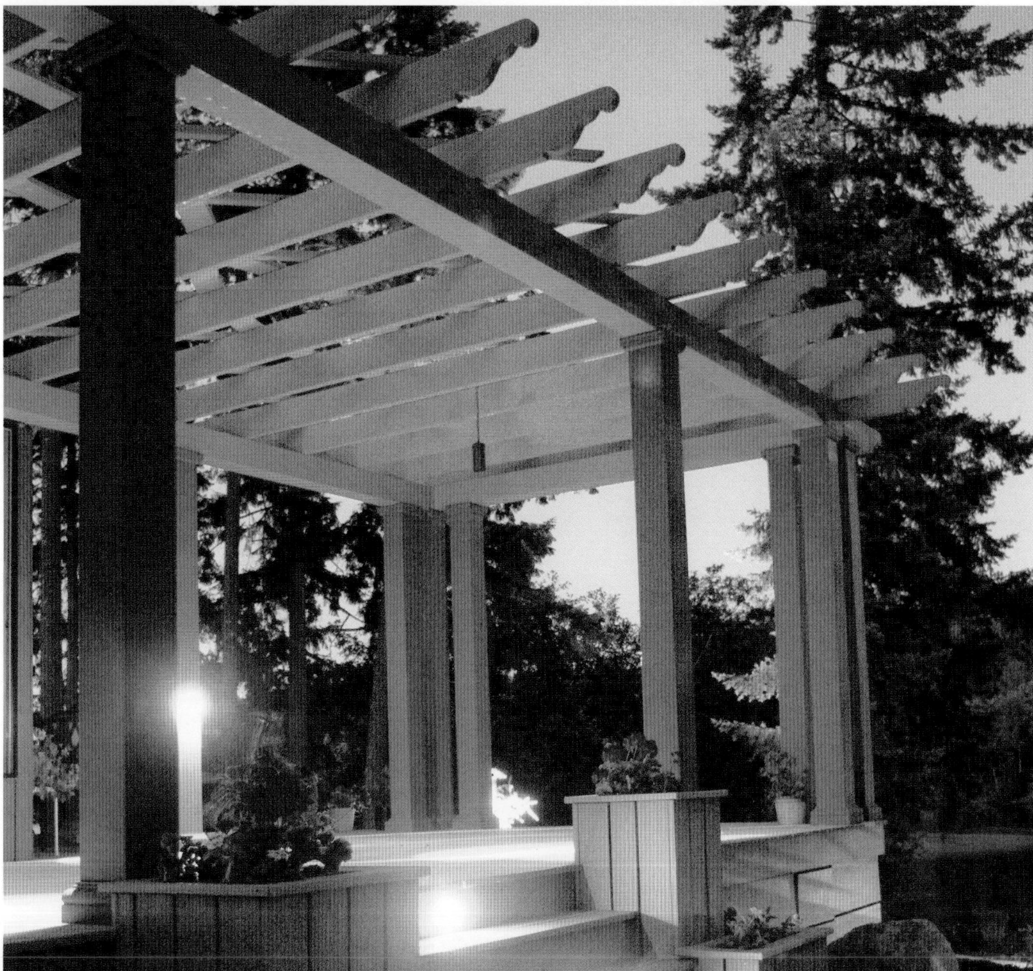

Light your pergola for drama. Pergolas are already captivating features on any deck, but never more so than when properly lit at night. This structure is evidence of how spectacular the features look when lit with a bit of theatrical insight. The lighting plays off the varied surfaces of the pergola's support structure and roof, creating a wonderful impression that is stage-like in its look.

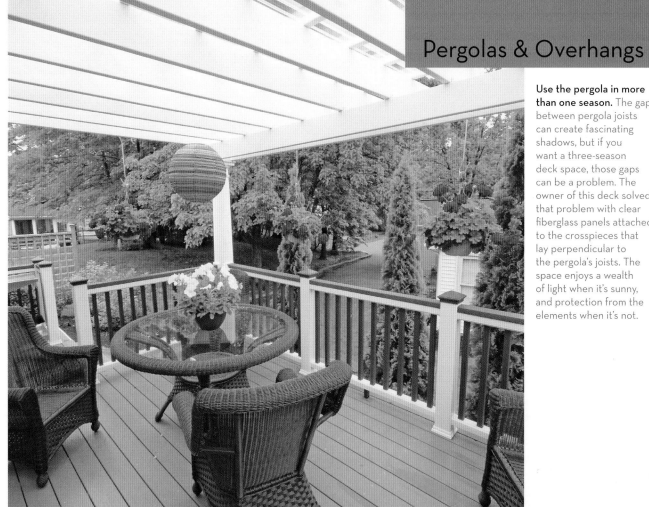

Outfit your gazebo as an outdoor room. This was clearly the deck builder's idea in designing this gazebo, with sides that echo the white siding on the house, and a roof made of the same shingles as used on the house. It is an outdoor space that is at once part of the deck, and a standalone room where people can sit in more private and intimate surroundings.

Relax in total shade by screening-in your deck gazebo. This one was built from the same ipe hardwood used to construct the deck. By using the same wood on both deck and gazebo, the homeowner unified the appearance of the outdoor space, creating an appealing visual continuity.

Add a screened door and access stairs. This type of relationship requires a lot of planning in the interplay between deck and gazebo, and you need to be certain that your goal is a standalone exterior room rather than a slightly intimate area set to one side of the deck.

Roof for the right impression. This lovely gazebo provides a lounging oasis off to the side of the deck, but the feature that really ties it together with everything around it is the roof. Splitting the difference between the tones of the deck, house, and surrounding homes, the bleached white color and aged appearance make the gazebo fit in not only with the deck, but the neighborhood as well.

It's hip to be square. This square gazebo can more than hold its own against circular styles. The designer included decorative exterior corner panels and lattice skirting that surrounds not only the base of the gazebo, but the base of the deck as well. Skirting is a great way to block out the usually unsightly supports necessary to hold up a deck gazebo.

Dress up any deck with a formal gazebo. They are almost like tiny room additions. This intricate gazebo features custom balusters, a stacked pagoda roof, and gingerbread trim, all of which add up to an eye-catching package. Gray lattice skirting helps ground the structure and conceal the support posts that—if apparent—would have detracted from the overall look.

Create clear separation with a gazebo. This sprawling outdoor surface includes a spa tub with its own platform, an exposed dining area in the center of the deck, and a screened-in gazebo with its own door. Although each area is distinctly different, using the same wood throughout the deck tells the eye that all sections are part of a whole.

Gazebos

Nestle a gazebo into naturalistic surroundings. The gazebo on this deck has been situated on a slight peninsula, almost on top of a koi pond. The water feature adds a calm and peaceful element to the scene. No other area of the deck is better sited to enjoy the pond than this covered, meditative sitting space.

Complement a pool with a gazebo. The structure here offers open-air shade from the overwhelming midday sun and a place to dry off, eat, and relax in between swim sessions. It's essentially a compromise between getting too much sun on the deck and going inside. This particular gazebo also offers an ideal vantage point from which parents can supervise children playing in the pool.

Open up your gazebo for an even more unique look. A gazebo doesn't necessarily need to be a self-contained room. In the right situation, it can be a minimal and elegant accent. This deck addition is little more than supporting columns and an elegant roof over curving built-in benches. But the style, as restrained as it may be, perfectly suits the simple, traditional design of the rest of the deck.

Maximize air circulation and view. Allowing air and light to penetrate under a gazebo such as this helps head off any moisture-related problems such as mold or rot. It also lends the construction to easy inspection of the structural timbers, allowing for quick detection of any problems before they become serious.

Gazebos

Integrate a gazebo. Gazebos are often built to sit separately from the deck itself, but that doesn't have to be the case. The builder of this deck designed a single-level surface with the gazebo positioned for interaction with the other areas. People enjoying a drink in the gazebo can have a conversation with a group clustered around the stone fire pit, separate but still together.

Where the budget is big, go big with your gazebo. Traditional open-post supports or a skirting-enclosed structure are not the only options for a gazebo's base. The support itself can be an opportunity for creativity, as this unique deck clearly shows. The gazebo is supported on a one-of-a-kind poured cement foundation that creates its own attention-getting feature.

Light your gazebo for nighttime socializing and relaxing. Especially on overcast nights where the stars don't provide a reason for reclining on the deck, a gazebo can offer an intimate space with enough light for socializing, but with the outdoor connection no kitchen or living room can offer.

Use a privacy screen for more than one purpose. This beautiful, slatted ornamental fence—designed to match the graceful, slim pergola—not only contributes a stunning visual feature to the look of the deck, it also serves as a wind break for the fire pit. The practical application ensures the comfort of this social area while providing a lovely backdrop that creates a sense of intimacy.

Limit the exposure to a neighbors' yard. Square-pattern lattice effectively blocks prying eyes, while allowing for air circulation and light penetration. Using screens on both sides of the deck is a great idea in situations where the goal is to create an intimate feeling for the whole structure.

Privacy Screens & Fences

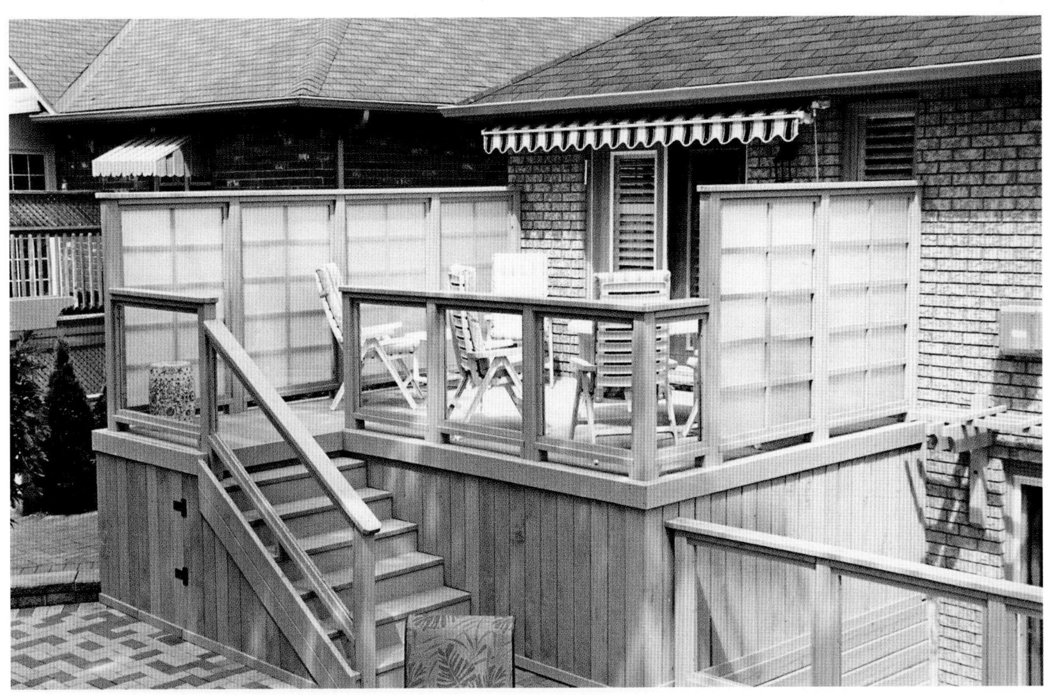

Achieve mental and physical separation. This house is almost connected to its neighbors, but the owner wanted some sense of having his own outdoor space. The solution was Japanese-style privacy screens created with simple squares of the same wood used in the deck, covered with exterior-grade fabric that is water- and UV-resistant.

Use stepped privacy screens for a sophisticated look. This simple, tight lattice pattern with a top rail flows visually into the elegant railing, which itself follows the gently curved shape of the deck. A large staircase planter box completes the design on the other side. The square lattice skirting mimics the look of the privacy screens and pulls the whole design together.

Contrast with a finely crafted privacy screen. The spa tub here was painted gray so that it would fade down into the deck. But the privacy screen was left natural so that the fine details of the staggered screen layout would stand out against the deck. Notice the handrails have been left natural as well, to carry through the look of the screen and lead the eye (as well as the visitor) up to the tub.

Create elegant, operable deck screens with outdoor fabric. Simple frames graced with drapes of water- and fade-resistant exterior fabric ensure that any time the owner of this deck wants an intimate outdoor dinner, it's easy to achieve. This is a great solution for any deck where the view is nice, but occasional privacy is a goal.

Privacy Screens & Fences

Add a charming element by installing lights on a privacy screen. The screens on this deck form a wall along the property line; post-mounted downlights make the pattern of the latticework pop out. Light bounces off the screen, creating a much more charming and inviting feel than if the deck had been left wide open.

Customize a privacy screen to suit specific needs. The fabric roller screens used on this deck provide a backdrop for the bartender servicing this outdoor bar on an elevated deck. The screens ensure intimacy for a summer evening cocktail party, but they are also very stylish. The lower portion of the wall doesn't need to be screened, because the bar itself blocks that part of a view. It's a very thoughtful, insightful approach to including a screen in deck design.

Dine discreetly with a solid dining-area privacy screen. Although any deck or deck area can be outfitted with a privacy screen, they are often most useful for dining areas. Nobody likes to be watched while eating, and adding a privacy screen around a dining table ensures that the atmosphere is kept cozy and social for memorable cookouts and outdoor dinner parties.

Privacy Screens & Fences

Let lattice serve your privacy needs. This simple, plain screen provides a modicum of privacy whether the homeowner is enjoying a weekend summer morning with the paper or hosting an intimate cookout party. The latticework seamlessly blends with other deck details because the builder used the same post style as in the railings on the deck.

Manufacture intimacy anywhere on the deck. This five-foot-tall screen isn't a formidable presence on the otherwise open deck, and it doesn't need to be. It effectively blocks a view of the street from the side of the deck and allows for contemplative rocking or a restful hour spent reading, away from the rest of the world.

Add the perfect centerpiece with a self-contained concrete fire pit. Framed with built-in benches and accented with cushions and throw pillows, this scene screams comfort. The pit is just large enough to warm and illuminate the area, and comes equipped with a copper hood that prevents embers from flying up and away. The hood can also be used to extinguish the fire when it's time to go inside.

Choose a fire pit that suits your tastes and your deck. Pits come in all shapes, sizes, and materials. Modest models simply supply a small flame, but larger, ornate units like the one shown here can serve as decorative centerpieces. Lit or unlit, this is an eye-catching feature, with its intricate wrought-metal base. The stone lip can hold a plate of food, a drink, or your feet while you warm them.

Fire Pits & Fireplaces

Create a comfortable social center. This is the basic idea behind all fire pits. The homeowner who outfitted this deck designed a perfect relaxation zone around a metal fire pit, with well-cushioned chairs and benches clustered together. Notice that the pit is covered with a safety screen to keep coals and embers off the composite decking and out of the hillside vegetation.

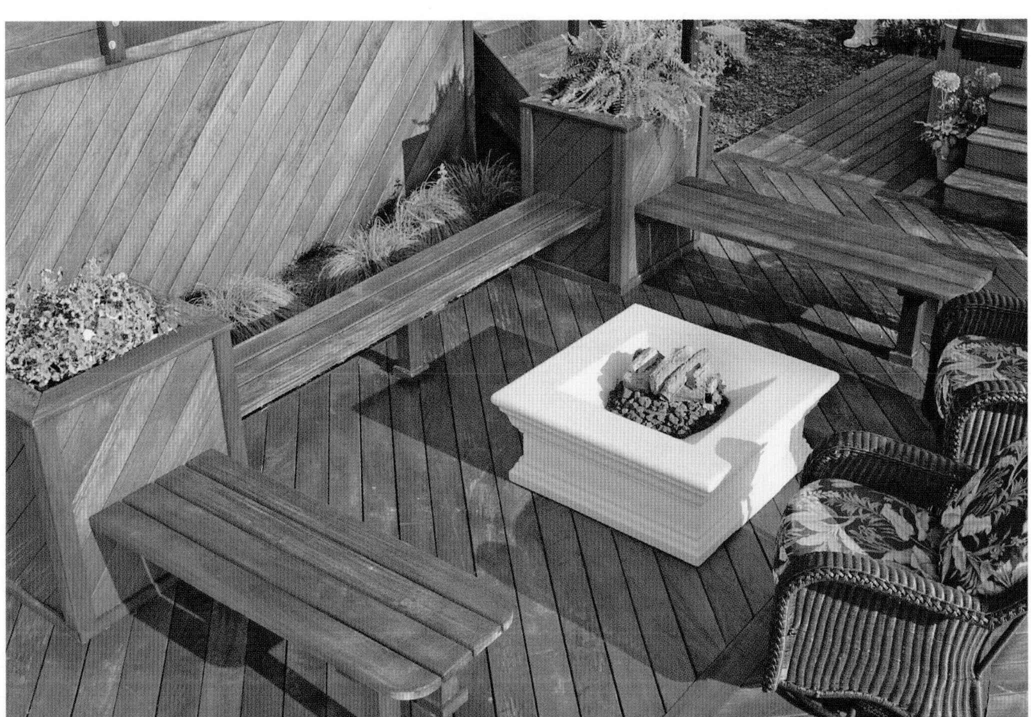

Create pleasant and flexible conversation circles. This configuration gives you maximum flexibility. The U-shaped built-in benches here were crafted specifically to cluster around the fire pit. The ceramic pit is arresting in its own right, and even more so with a lively orange blaze burning in the center.

Focus on a one-of-kind fire pit. This spectacular multilevel deck curves around an equally spectacular stacked-stone fire pit. The white stone perfectly complements the two-tone composite decking and provides an obvious focal point. Built-in seating curves invitingly around the fire pit, and underseat lighting supplements the illumination from the pit.

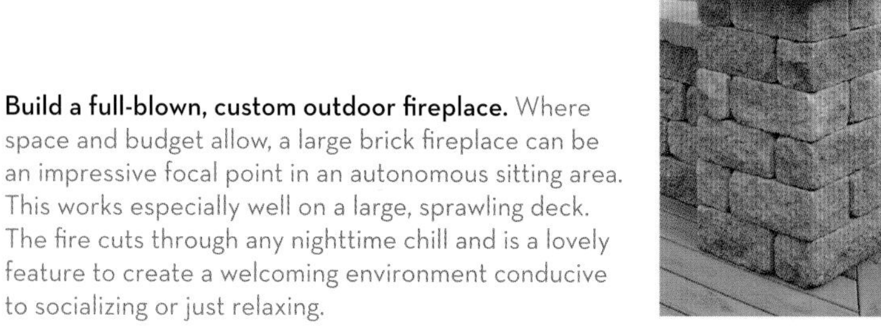

Build a full-blown, custom outdoor fireplace. Where space and budget allow, a large brick fireplace can be an impressive focal point in an autonomous sitting area. This works especially well on a large, sprawling deck. The fire cuts through any nighttime chill and is a lovely feature to create a welcoming environment conducive to socializing or just relaxing.

Fire Pits & Fireplaces

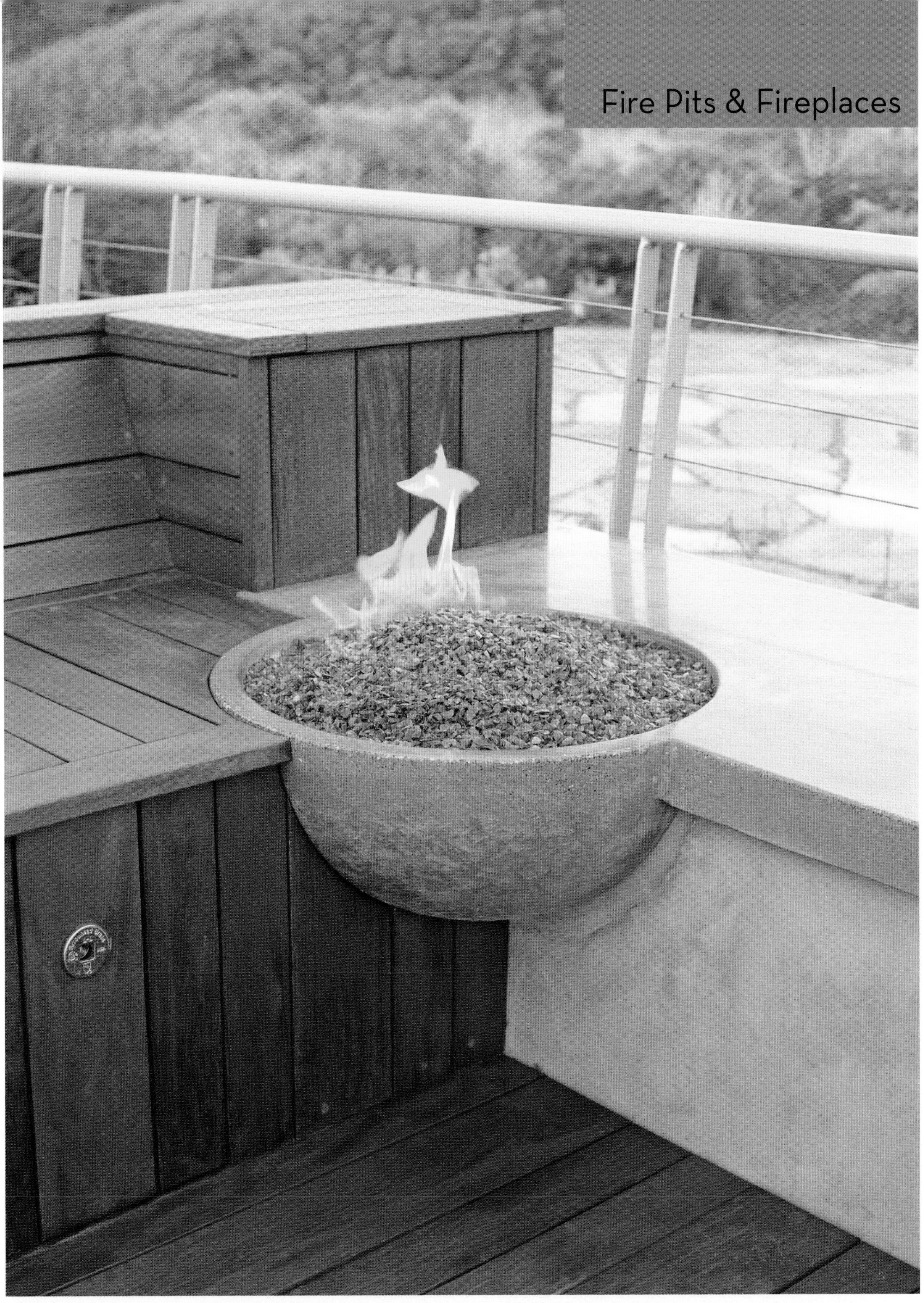

Think outside the box for an incredible and opulent deck feature. Rather than incorporate a traditional fire pit in the center of this deck, the builder customized one into the concrete bench. It's a sleek treatment that allows people to snug right up close to the fire and still enjoy the built-in seating.

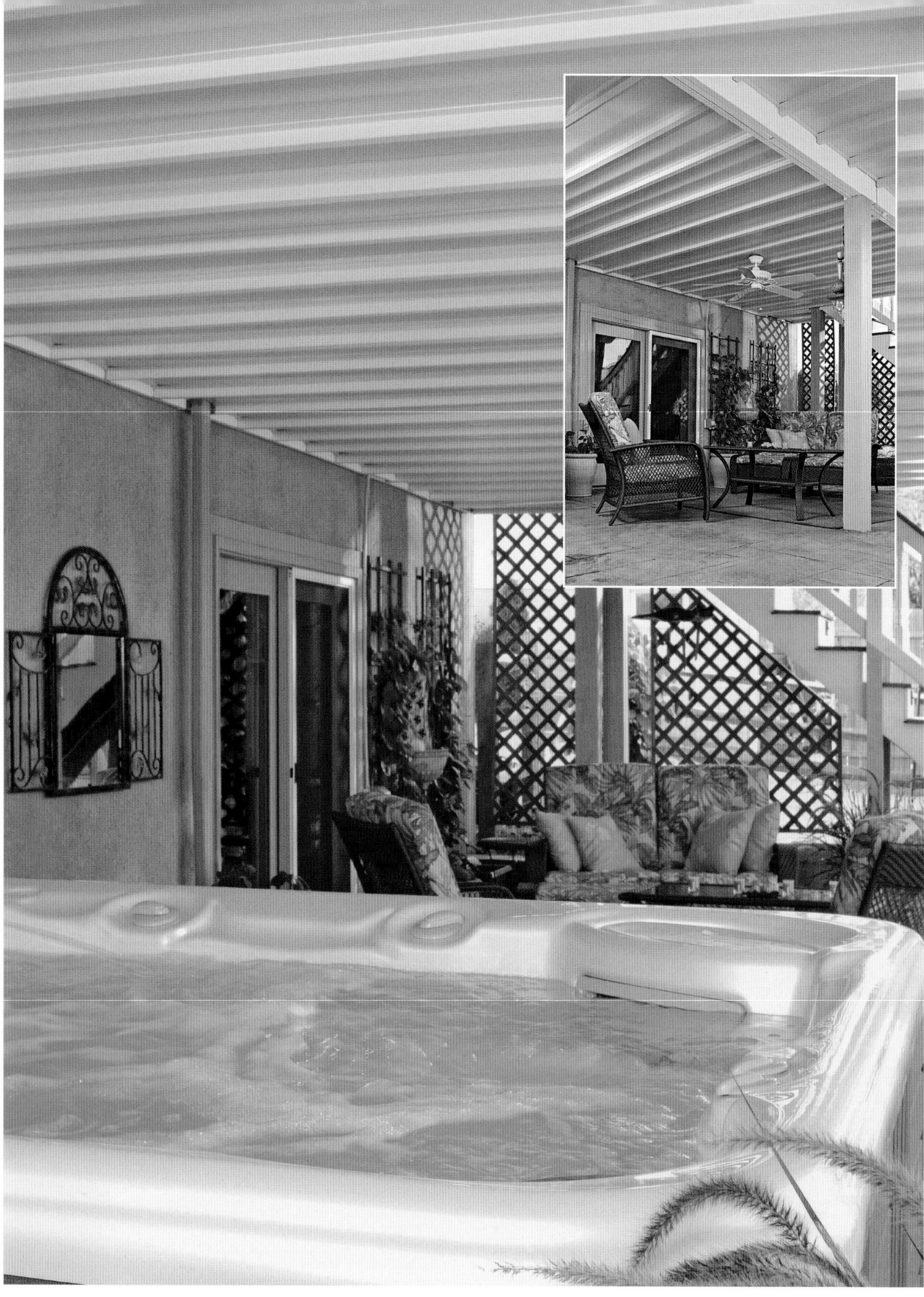

Tap new technology to make use of the space underneath a deck. The manufacturer of this system offers everything you'll need to enclose the space between joists and make the space waterproof. The system includes brackets and U-shaped vinyl channels that are fairly easy to install. The channels direct rainwater to troughs that then channel it to the ground. It's a wonderful way to make a dry, shady outdoor room to complement any elevated deck.

Underdeck Spaces

Create a shaded sitting area. With the help of a prefab vinyl capping system that encloses the space between deck joists, this outdoor sitting area has been expanded to run underneath the elevated deck, making good use of space that would otherwise be left bare and empty. Systems such as these are offered by a limited number of deck manufacturers.

Improve an underdeck area for a custom look. This patio extends under an elevated deck, which would have normally translated to lost space. But the builder clad the underside of the deck, added waterproofed blocking between the joists, and installed recessed lighting. The result is a lovely sitting area that can be used at night.

DECK LIGHTING

The lighting fixtures you incorporate into your deck are essential safety features. A well-lit deck can head off trips and falls, simple missteps, and other accidents. Step lighting, for instance, is crucial on an elevated deck used for nighttime cookouts. Because most decks are attached to the home and lead to a back door, deck lights are also often a first line of defense against intruders. The lights chosen to illuminate your deck should take these vital functions into account.

But deck lighting is so much more than safety and practicality. It can also serve as a high-impact decorative element. This is true of both the illumination and the lighting fixtures themselves. Where and how you direct light over different parts of a deck can create moods from bright, lively, and fun to romantic and mysterious. You'll find lighting fixtures that sparkle with their own verve, or you can choose other types designed to blend into the deck's structure.

Regardless of the look or light you're after, you'll be presented with an amazing array of ever-increasing options, thanks to innovative manufacturers. The options represent an incredible diversity of styles, power source, and potential placements.

Solar fixtures are exploding in popularity because they not only add nothing to your electricity bill, they can also be placed just about anywhere on the deck that gets a good amount of sun during the day. Low-voltage lights are also useful because they can be plugged and unplugged into an outdoor outlet, making it easy to relocate them. Wired-in fixtures are best used on larger or more complex decks where the expense will be justified in relation to the overall construction cost. No matter what lighting you select, make sure that both the fixtures and the illumination they provide show your deck off to its best advantage.

Outfit complex, multilevel, or large decks with a thoughtfully balanced blend of lighting. This stunning deck is an example of mixing and matching lighting to suit purpose and provide just the right amount of illumination. Step-riser lights make walking off or onto the deck in the dark a trouble-free experience. Post-cap lights help define the perimeter of the deck without flooding the area with distracting light. The mix of lighting combines to showcase the deck's design to its best advantage after dark.

Opt for maximum adaptability with post-mounted and baluster-mounted lights. Post-mounted lights can usually be installed on any side of the post and at any height, whatever placement suits your preferences. Baluster lights are even more adaptable, because they can be placed anywhere along a railing. In both of the examples shown, the fixtures are meant to seamlessly blend into the railing, with hoods that match the color and material of the surrounding structure, and direct the beam of light down, not into people's eyes.

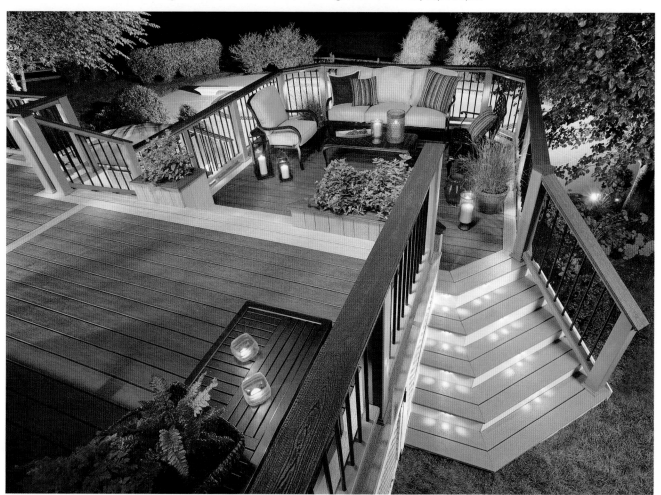

Integrate deck lighting with a larger yard lighting plan. You choice of deck fixtures should take into account ambient sources of nighttime illumination. This poolside deck incorporates modest fixtures under handrails and stair lighting for safety. No other lights are necessary because sufficient ambient light is supplied by the dramatic uplights under the trees, the pool lights, and the light that pours out of the home's large windows.

Decorate your deck posts with a totally unique post-cap light fixture. The pyramid shape of these light fixture crowns is fairly common because it sheds water efficiently. But that's the only common thing about these fixtures. The surface of both features a hand-wrought hammered relief, in an antique black finish on one, and a glossy red "oxidized" look for its brother. Manufacturers are constantly diversifying their fixture styles into new and eye-catching designs. It only makes sense to find one that complements your particular deck.

Opt for understatement with a partially concealed fixture. Although there are a bevy of deck lighting fixture designs that you can use for both illumination and ornamentation, if you want the wood—such as the redwood in this deck—to take center stage, you'd be wise to choose subtle fixtures that are all about the light. This under-rail light directs illumination down to the deck, increasing safety without calling attention to itself.

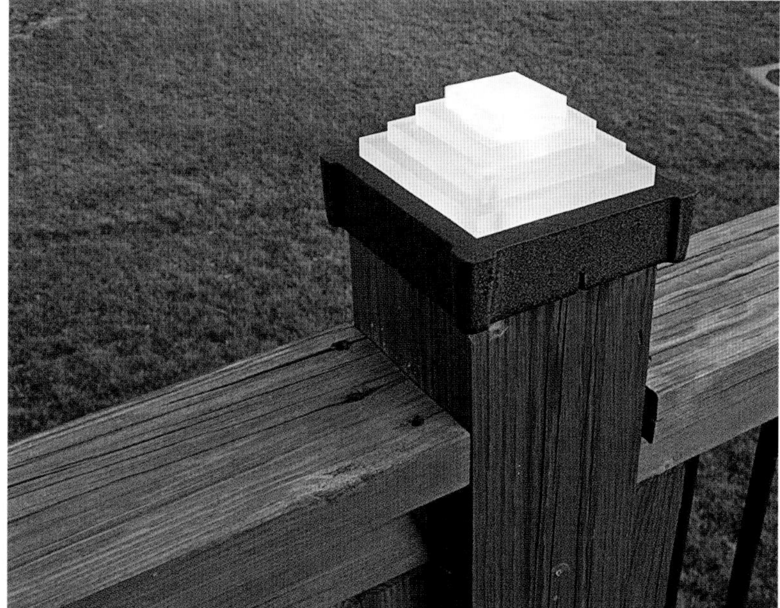

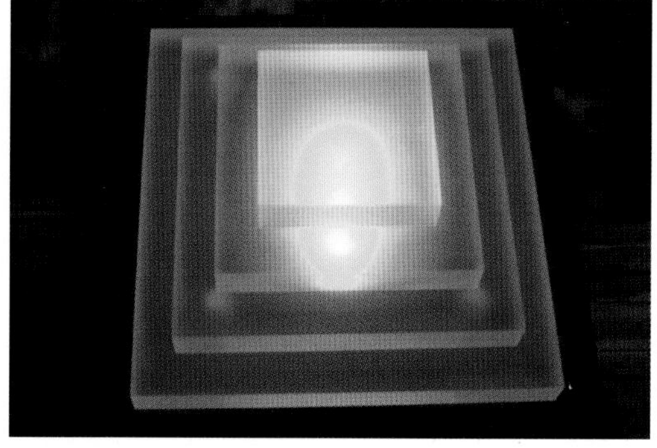

Introduce a changeable element by using high-profile translucent fixture. This pyramid stack of plastic squares forms a spectacular post-top light that draws the eye both during the day, and after dark. In sunlight, it's plain white and handsome. At night, the center block glows with focused illumination—in this case, in an appealing yellow. The bulb can be changed to, for instance, a baby blue or another color.

Choose post cap finishes wisely. You'll find post-cap fixtures in different finishes and a limited range of colors. The look you choose should either intentionally contrast (the sharp look of black against a light wood post) or complement (a gray fixture that blends into the construction of the deck) the rest of the deck. Consider railings, posts, other lighting fixtures and the landscape in your decision.

Use multidirectional light. The post-side light fixture here is an accent feature during the day—the metal finish matches the post-cap fixture material—and dazzles at night with a patterned lighting that supplements the lighting from the post cap. It's a fascinating look that provides ample illumination.

Don't over-illuminate. In deck lighting, less is often more. These steps, leading from a small porch to a larger deck, need only indicators of step location and depth. Being so close to the house, there is plenty of ambient lighting. The small, integrated spots work better than more elaborate, brighter fixtures would.

Keep lighting subtle. The simple combination of understated lighting works perfectly with the integral pool and jetted spa lights to insure against slips on this deck. But by showing a bit of restraint in the number and power of supplementary fixtures, the lighting doesn't kill the romantic and slightly mysterious appearance that makes water features so alluring at night.

Deck Lighting

Allow a nighttime view to dominate by using downlighting. Downlights, like the rail lights on this deck, project illumination at the deck itself, providing safety for moving around but without intruding on the beauty of a star-filled sky or colorful sunset.

Wire freestanding deck structures to create cozy enclaves. The pavilion that graces this deck has been wired for power, allowing for sconces, adjustable spotlights, and a fan-light combination. Each set of lights is wired to a different switch so that the host can control the mood and effectiveness of the lighting and accommodate different times and conditions (such as a moonless night).

Take advantage of new options. The sandblasted glass panels in this deck's barrier rails are attractive enough on their own, but the design in the glass really comes to life when lit by a simple rail uplight. This technique would be perfect to create a truly memorable railing, or anywhere you have a vertical element on your deck. Just make sure the glass panels meet all safety regulations and that they are correctly secured in place.

Think outside the box. Although the most common addition to make stairs safer at night is tread-riser lights, this staircase makes good use of a wonderful product—decorative baluster lights. The lights look like sparkling gems suspended in the railings but—more importantly—they provide all the wattage necessary to make the stairs completely safe, even on a moonless night.

Lead the eye with lighting. Deck lighting, especially stair lighting, can be a wonderful way to lead the eye where you want the viewer to go. The riser spotlights installed in this staircase not only make climbing a fairly steep structure safer, they also lead the eye up and create a visual sense of anticipation of what's at the top of the stairs. This is the same principle used in pathway lighting and can be very effective in deck design.

Match post-side lamps to the railing style. The black balusters in this deck railing are an interesting visual all on their own, and they are perfectly complemented by the punctuation points of simple round post lights spaced evenly across the deck. The lights provide necessary downlighting, but also add a nice graphic touch that fits right in with the deck's overall design.

Leverage contemporary technology. Small, pinpoint recessed lights installed right into deck boards can be placed just about anywhere on the deck surface and can serve a specific function such as a pathway to a door or stairs, or simply be an interesting element underfoot.

Deck Lighting

Signal sophistication with small touches. Stair-step lights serve a vital safety function, but that's why they are often overlooked when it comes to graphic potential. A stylish shape and appealing metal finish can make these tiny fixtures worth a look of their own, and add even more style to your steps.

Make an informed selection of deck lighting. The owners of this deck chose to add neon strips around the top of the gazebo and privacy fence. The added light doesn't produce much illumination for the deck, but it does add an intriguing splash of glowing color at eye level.

Conceal deck lighting for an unobtrusive element. Deck lighting fixtures should not detract from the overall look of the deck during the day. Miniature recessed under-rail lights, like the one on the bottom of this handrail, light the way on a set of steps with an almost mysterious illumination. This type of hidden light is ideal for a modern look on a deck that features sleek lines and cutting-edge materials.

Tap the amazing variety of deck lighting fixtures. The recessed, low-voltage mini spotlights shown in this deck are most commonly used as staircase lights. But they make wonderful accents when used to light a path across the deck. It's a great way to add some fun and an unexpected element to an otherwise sedate deck design.

Deck Lighting

Install stair-step lighting for safe climbing. The riser spotlights used on these steps are subtle, but they provide enough light to illuminate the differences in tread depths. The extremely subdued post-cap lights also serve as visual indicators of the step-down. Notice that the lighting is all very modest, preserving the quiet mood of an evening on the deck.

Use geometry in art glass. This lovely stained glass fixture is comprised of linear pieces of glass, forming a design that is neatly organized and well-suited as post-top decoration and lighting.

Create a mood and improve safety. Although post-cap fixtures are usually used on transition posts throughout the deck, the designer of this deck used solar-powered fixtures on every post, along with spotlights on the step risers. The spots are connected to the deck's weatherproof outdoor electrical outlet and controlled by an electronic eye that senses when the sun goes down.

Satisfy a preference for subtlety. These modest fixtures look like a solid, milled post cap in the light of day. But at night, the lighting integrated on the underside of the lip provides soft illumination that ensures safety on steps and a lighted path anywhere else. This type of post-cap lighting is the height of sophistication and understatement.

Sometimes the choice is black and white. The black post-cap lighting fixture (left) will blend into the nighttime landscape and is a more somber look. It is best suited where the landscaping is dense and the wood or furniture on the deck is darker in hue. Opt for a white cap (right) for a cleaner, brighter appearance that will stand out in the dark. In either case, the textured glass inserts add a ton of visual interest day or night.

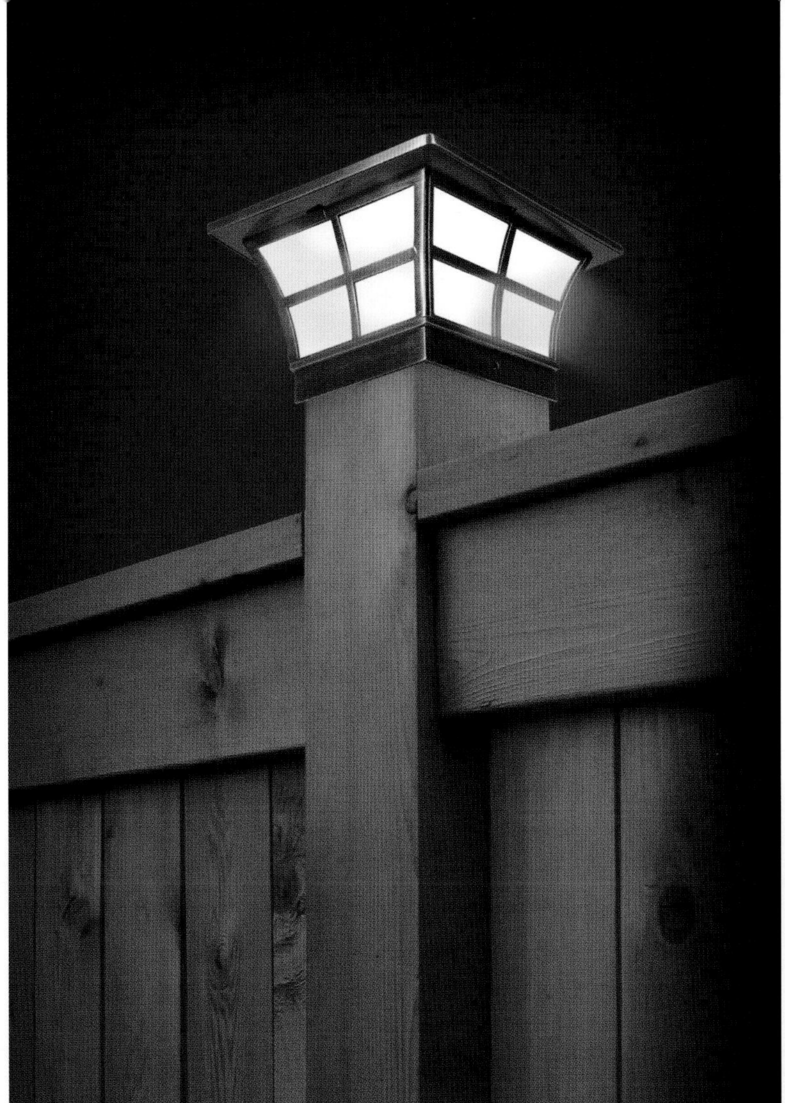

Deck Lighting

Pair natural metal with natural wood for a stunning look. This copper fixture marries perfectly with the natural cedar deck privacy fence. Not only are the shades compatible, the flare of the light fixture seems like a natural extension and completion of the post shape. Keep in mind that unless they have been finished with sealant, natural metal fixtures will eventually collect a patina of oxidation. Copper, for instance, will age to a very attractive light jade green left untreated.

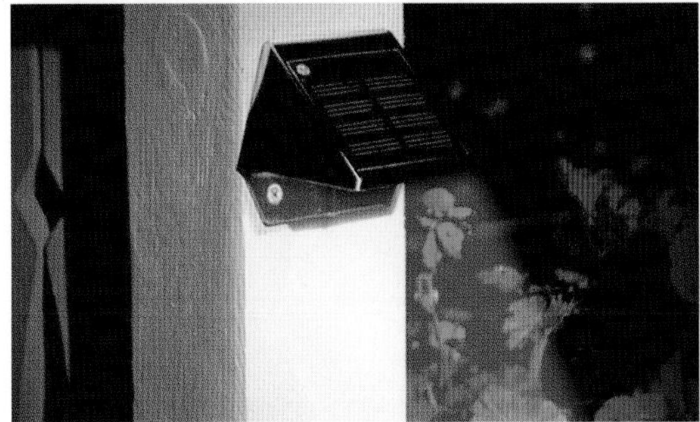

Select solar, go-anywhere lighting. Don't want to deal with wiring or routing lighting near an outlet? Then turn to the ever-increasing number of solar post, post-cap, and stairway lighting options. These range from the eminently practical to the beautifully artful. The wedge-shaped post light (above) provides a surprising illumination along the base of the post, and is easily installed with a drill and screwdriver. The integrated solar post cap light (right) is an example of how beautiful these fixtures can be—it's hard to tell this is a solar fixture and not a custom-milled piece.

Deck Lighting

Mix accent lighting with ambient light. This multilevel structure was installed on the side of a home, away from any ambient lights. Consequently, the designer used bright post-mounted lights for general lighting, post-cap lights to mark step downs, and recessed stair-riser spots that reveal step depths in the darkness.

Integrate portable or freestanding lighting. A variety of candle lanterns and an unwired lamppost provide basic, romantic, and functional lighting for a small deck. The placement of these fixtures on the steps is not only artful, it ensures against tripping on the steps in the dark. The fixtures themselves become part of the artistry of the deck and blend perfectly with the thick, bushy jungle fauna surrounding the deck.

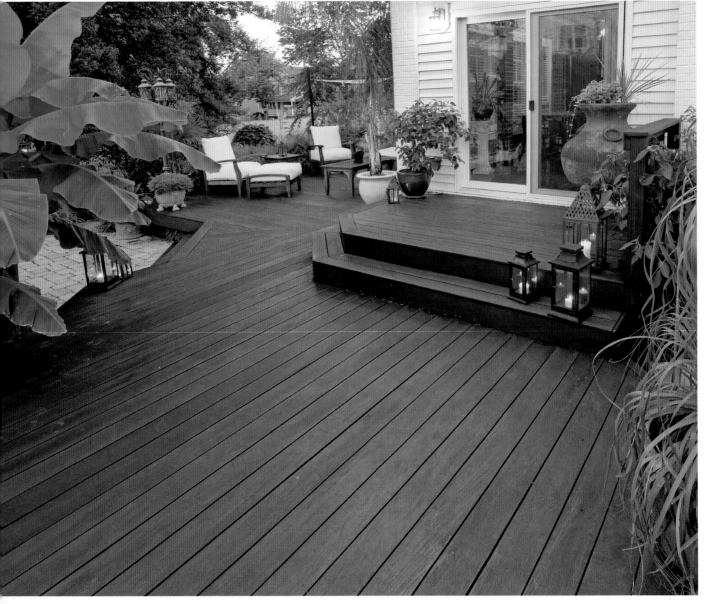

Photo Credits

Photos courtesy of 4 Quarters Design & Build, www.4qdb.com: 18 (both), 19 (both)

Photos courtesy of Advantage Trim and Lumber Company, www.advantagelumber.com: 26, 27 (both), 28 (both), 29 (bottom), 38 (top), 83, 86, 87 (bottom), 125 (top), 142 (bottom), 157

Photos courtesy of Archadeck, www.archadeck.com, (888) OUR-DECK: 9 (bottom), 58 (bottom), 63 (bottom), 78 (top), 82 (bottom), 101 (top), 156 (bottom)

Photos courtesy of Aurora Deck Lighting, www.auroradecklighting.com: 73 (bottom), 152

Photos courtesy Azek, www.azek.com: 4, 16, 42 (bottom), 43 (all), 44 (bottom), 45 (both), 54 (top), 57 (bottom right), 61 (both), 66 (bottom), 75 (bottom), 80, 125, 135 (bottom)

Photos courtesy of Bruno, www.bruno.com: 105 (both)

Photos courtesy of California Redwood Association, www.calredwood.org

photos by Ernest Braun: 12 (top), 18 (top), 19 (top), 21 (top), 124,

photos by Charles Callister, Jr.: 17 (both), 21 (bottom),

photos by Mark Becker: 18 (bottom), 77

photos by Robert Perron: 20 (top)

photos by Jeffrey Rycus: 20 (bottom), 57 (bottom left)

photos by Vic Moss: 84 (top)

photos by Marvin Sloben: 88 (left)

Photos courtesy of Cal Spas, www.calspas.com: 10 (top), 81 (top), 84 (bottom)

Photos courtesy of CertainTeed Corporation, www.certainteed.com: 5 (bottom), 6 (bottom), 64, 69 (bottom), 88 (right)

Photos courtesy of Classy Caps Mfg, Inc., www.fencecaps.com, (866) 460-4604: 171 (bottom right), 172 (all), 173 (all)

Photos courtesy of Clemens Jellema, Fine Decks, Inc., www.finedecks.com: 7 (top), 11 (top), 29 (top), 63 (top), 66 (top), 67 (bottom), 68 (top), 71 (both), 72 (both), 75 (top), 76 (both), 78 (bottom), 95 (top), 97 (both), 98, 99 (top), 102 (top), 107 (both), 108 (top), 110 (both), 111 (bottom), 113 (top), 115 (both), 116 (top), 117 (bottom), 118 (both), 119 (both), 120 (both), 121 (both), 129 (both), 130 (top), 131 (bottom), 132, 134 (top), 136 (bottom), 138 (top), 139, 140 (bottom), 141 (top), 142 (top), 143 (top left, bottom), 151 (bottom), 153 (both), 154 (bottom), 155 (bottom), 159 (bottom), 165 (bottom), 168 (top), 174 (bottom)

Photos courtesy of Clubhouse Decking by Deceuninck, www.clubhousedecking.com: 13 (top), 15 (bottom), 143 (bottom)

Photos courtesy of The Deck & Door Company (www.deckanddoor.com): 55 (bottom), 108 (bottom), 109 (bottom), 114 (left), 137 (top)

Photos courtesy of Deckbuilders, www.nicedeck.com, (256) 679-8494: 104 (both)

Photos courtesy of Deck Builders, Inc., www.artistryindecks.com: 53 (top), 96 (bottom), 99 (bottom) 126 (top), 133 (bottom), 141 (bottom)

Photo courtesy of Decklighting Systems, www.decklightingsystems.com: 70 (top), 161, 165 (top)

Photos courtesy of Deck Specialists, www.deckspecialists.com: 24 (bottom), 25 (bottom)

Photos courtesy of Dekor, www.de-kor.com: 164 (all), 166 (all), 167, 170 (both), 174 (top)

Photos courtesy of Duradek, www.duradek.com, (800) 338-3568: 7 (bottom), 50 (both), 51 (both), 116 (bottom), 117 (top, middle)

Photos courtesy of DuraLife™ Decking & Railing Systems, www.duralifedecking.com, (800) 866-8101: 14 (top), 33, 36 (both), 38 (all), 39 (bottom), 56 (bottom), 57 (top), 62, 113 (bottom), 134 (bottom)

Photos courtesy of Fiberon Composite Decking, www.fiberondecking.com: 6 (top), 26 (both), 34 (top), 58 (top), 65, 79 (both), 85, 106, 155 (top)

Photos courtesy of Fortress Iron Railing & Fence Systems, www.fortressiron.com: 59 (left), 68 (bottom), 109 (top), 126 (bottom), 133 (top)

Photos courtesy of GAF Decking Systems, www.gaf.com: 67 (top), 73 (top), 89

Photos courtesy of Gossen Corporation, www.gossencorp.com, (800) 558-8984: 14 (bottom), 44 (top)

Photos courtesy of HandyDeck Systems Inc., www.handydeck.com: 48 (both), 49 (all)

Photos courtesy of Hickory Dickory Decks, www.hickorydickorydecks.com, (800) 263-4774: 90 (bottom), 91 (both), 92 (both), 95 (bottom), 96 (top), 123 (top), 128, 130 (bottom), 131 (top), 135 (top), 136 (top), 140 (top), 144 (both), 145 (both), 146 (bottom), 147 (all), 148 (both), 149 (both), 150 (top), 151 (top), 169 (bottom)

Photos courtesy of Ironwoods: 30 (both), 31 (both), 59 (right)

iStock: 90 (top), 93 (bottom), 102 (bottom)

Photos courtesy of Last-Deck, Inc., www.lastdeck.com: 46 (both), 47 (both)

Photo courtesy of Michal Gerard Construction, www.michalgerardconstruction.com: 101 (bottom)

Photos courtesy of MoistureShield, www. moistureshield.com, (866) 729-2378: 9 (top), 40 (bottom), 87 (top), 93 (top)

Photos courtesy of Moonlight Decks, LLC, www.moonlightdecks.com, (913) 638-1685: 162 (all), 163 (all)

Photos courtesy of Nyloboard, nyloboard.com, (877) 695-6909: 15 (top), 82 (top)

Photos courtesy of RailingWorks, www.railingworks.com: 69 (top), 111 (top)

Photo courtesy of Rhino Deck, www.rhinodeck.com: 28 (bottom)

Photos courtesy of Simpson Strong-Tie, www.strongtie.com: 60 (both)

Shutterstock: 19 (bottom)

Photos courtesy of The Southern Pine Council, www.southernpinedecks.com: 24 (top), 25 (top)

Photo courtesy of Sundance Spas, www.sundancespas.com: 81 (bottom)

Photos courtesy of TAMKO Building Products, Inc., www.evergrain.com: 8, 12 (bottom), 55 (top), 94, 103 (bottom), 122, 154 (top)

Photos courtesy of TimberTech, www.timbertech.com: 10 (bottom), 11 (bottom), 13 (bottom), 35 (top right, bottom), 39 (top), 40 (top), 41 (both), 54 (bottom), 70 (bottom), 74, 103 (top), 112, 114 (right), 123 (bottom), 127 (top), 150 (bottom), 158 (both), 159 (top), 160, 161 (top, both), 169 (top)

Photos courtesy of Trex Company, Inc., www.trex.com: cover, 5 (top), 34 (bottom), 35 (top left), 53 (bottom), 100, 138 (bottom), 146 (top), 156 (top), 168 (bottom)

Photos courtesy of Universal Forest Products, Inc./Latitudes Decking, www.latitudesdeck.com: 37, 127 (bottom), 137 (bottom), 171 (all)

Resources

Archadeck
(888) OUR-DECK; www.archadeck.com

Aurora Deck Lighting
(800) 603-3520; www.auroradecklighting.com

Azek
(877) ASK-AZEK; www.azek.com

Bruno
www.bruno.com

Cal Spas
(800) CAL-SPAS; www.calspas.com

California Redwood Council
www.calredwood.org

CertainTeed Corporation
(800) 782-8777; www.certainteed.com

ChoiceDek
(800) 951-5117; www.choicedek.com

Classy Caps
(866) 460.4604; www.fencecaps.com

Correct Deck/GAF Decking Systems
(877) 332-5877; www.correctdeck.com

Deck Lighting Systems
(888) 305-4232; www.decklightingsystems.com

Dekor
(800) 258-0344; www.de-kor.com

Duradek
www.duradek.com

Duralife
(800) 866-8101; www.duralifedecking.com

Fiberon
(800) 573-8841; www.fiberondecking.com

Forest Stewardship Council
(612) 353-4511; www.fscus.org

Fortress Iron Railing & Fence Systems
(866) 323-4766; www.fortressiron.com

HandyDeck/EzyTile
(888) 681-2072; www.ezytile.com

Highpoint Deck Lighting
(888) 582-5850; www.hpdlighting.com

Iron Woods
(888) 932-9663; ironwoods.com

Jacuzzi
(866) 234-7727; www.jacuzzi.com

Last Deck
(866) 527-8332; www.lastdeck.com

LockDry/FSI Home Products
(888) 739-6172; www.lockdry.com

MoistureShield
(866) 729-2378; www.moistureshield.com

Moonlight Decks
(913) 638-1685; www.moonlightdecks.com

NADRA (North American Deck and Railing Association)
(215) 679-4884; www.nadra.org

NyloBoard
(877) 695-6909; nyloboard.com

Rhino Deck
(800) 535-4838; www.rhinodeck.com

Simpson Strong-Tie
(800) 999-5099; www.strongtie.com

Southern Pine Council
(504) 443-4464; www.southernpine.com

Sundance Spas
(800) 883-7727; www.sundancespas.com

Tamko Building Products/Evergrain Decking
(800) 641-4691; www.tamko.com

TimberTech
800-307-7780; www.timbertech.com

Trex
(800) BUY-TREX; www.trex.com

United Forest Products/Latitudes Decking
(877) 463-8379; www.ufpi.com